# The FIRST 100

# CHINESE CHARACTERS

**The quick and easy way to learn the basic Chinese characters**

**SIMPLIFIED** CHARACTER EDITION

Introduction by
Alison and Laurence Matthews

TUTTLE Publishing

Tokyo | Rutland, Vermont | Singapore

## "Books to Span the East and West"

**Tuttle Publishing** was founded in 1832 in the small New England town of Rutland, Vermont [USA]. Our core values remain as strong today as they were then—to publish best-in-class books which bring people together one page at a time. In 1948, we established a publishing office in Japan—and Tuttle is now a leader in publishing English-language books about the arts, languages and cultures of Asia. The world has become a much smaller place today and Asia's economic and cultural influence has grown. Yet the need for meaningful dialogue and information about this diverse region has never been greater. Over the past seven decades, Tuttle has published thousands of books on subjects ranging from martial arts and paper crafts to language learning and literature—and our talented authors, illustrators, designers and photographers have won many prestigious awards. We welcome you to explore the wealth of information available on Asia at **www.tuttlepublishing.com**.

Published by Tuttle Publishing, an imprint of Periplus Editions (HK) Ltd.

**www.tuttlepublishing.com**

LCC Card No. 2009387018
ISBN 978-0-8048-4992-0
(Published previously under 978-0-8048-3830-6)

**Distributed by:**

**North America, Latin America & Europe**
Tuttle Publishing, 364 Innovation Drive
North Clarendon, VT 05759-9436
Tel: 1 (802) 773 8930; Fax: 1 (802) 773 6993
info@tuttlepublishing.com
www.tuttlepublishing.com

**Japan**
Tuttle Publishing, Yaekari Building 3F 5-4-12 Osaki,
Shinagawa-ku Tokyo 141-0032, Japan
Tel: (81) 3 5437 0171; Fax: (81) 3 5437 0755
sales@tuttle.co.jp
www.tuttle.co.jp

**Asia-Pacific**
Berkeley Books Pte Ltd, 3 Kallang Sector #04-01/02
Singapore 349278
Tel: (65) 6741-2178; Fax: (65) 6741-2179
inquiries@periplus.com.sg
www.tuttlepublishing.com

25 24 23 22    10 9 8 7 6    2112TP
Printed in Singapore

TUTTLE PUBLISHING® is a registered trademark of Tuttle Publishing, a division of Periplus Editions (HK) Ltd.

# Contents

# Introduction

Learning the characters is one of the most fascinating and fun parts of learning Chinese, and people are often surprised by how much they enjoy being able to recognize them and to write them. Added to that, *writing* the characters is also the best way of *learning* them. This book shows you how to write the second 100 most common characters and gives you plenty of space to practice writing them. When you do this, you'll be learning a writing system which is one of the oldest in the world and is now used by more than a billion people around the globe every day.

In this introduction we'll talk about:
- how the characters developed;
- the difference between traditional and simplified forms of the characters;
- what the "radicals" are and why they're useful;
- how to count the writing strokes used to form each character;
- how to look up the characters in a dictionary;
- how words are created by joining two characters together; and, most importantly;
- how to write the characters!

Also, in case you're using this book on your own without a teacher, we'll tell you how to get the most out of using it.

Chinese characters are not nearly as strange and complicated as people seem to think. They're actually no more mysterious than musical notation, which most people can master in only a few months. So there's really nothing to be scared of or worried about: everyone can learn them—it just requires a bit of patience and perseverance. There are also some things which you may have heard about writing Chinese characters that aren't true. In particular, you don't need to use a special brush to write them (a ball-point pen is fine), and you don't need to be good at drawing (in fact you don't even need to have neat handwriting, although it helps!).

## How many characters are there?

Thousands! You would probably need to know something like two thousand to be able to read Chinese newspapers and books, but you don't need anything like that number to read a menu, go shopping or read simple street signs and instructions. Just as you can get by in most countries knowing about a hundred words of the local language, so too you can get by in China quite well knowing a hundred

common Chinese characters. And this would also be an excellent basis for learning to read and write Chinese.

## How did the characters originally develop?

Chinese characters started out as pictures representing simple objects, and the first characters originally resembled the things they represented. For example:

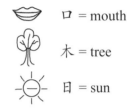

口 = mouth

木 = tree

日 = sun

Some other simple characters were pictures of "ideas":

一 one        二 two        三 three

Some of these characters kept this "pictographic" or "ideographic" quality about them, but others were gradually modified or abbreviated until many of them now look nothing like the original objects or ideas.

Then, as words were needed for things which weren't easy to draw, existing characters were "combined" to create new characters. For example, 女 (meaning "woman") combined with 子 (meaning "child") gives a new character 好 (which means "good" or "to be fond of").

Notice that when two characters are joined together like this to form a new character, they get squashed together and deformed slightly. This is so that the new, combined character will fit into the same size square or "box" as each of the original two characters. For example the character 日 "sun" becomes thinner when it is the left-hand part of the character 时 "time"; and it becomes shorter when it is the upper part of the character 星 "star". Some components got distorted and deformed even more than this in the combining process: for example when the character 人 "man" appears on the left-hand side of a complex character it gets compressed into 亻, like in the character 他 "he".

So you can see that some of the simpler characters often act as basic "building blocks" from which more complex characters are formed. This means that if you learn how to write these simple characters you'll also be learning how to write some complex ones too.

**How are characters read and pronounced?**

The pronunciations in this workbook refer to modern standard Chinese. This is the official language of China and is also known as "Mandarin" or "**putonghua**".

The pronunciation of Chinese characters is written out with letters of the alphabet using a romanization system called "Hanyu Pinyin"—or "**pinyin**" for short. This is the modern system used in China. In pinyin some of the letters have a different sound than in English—but if you are learning Chinese you'll already know this. We could give a description here of how to pronounce each sound, but it would take up a lot of space—and this workbook is about writing the characters, not pronouncing them! In any case, you really need to hear a teacher (or recording) pronounce the sounds out loud to get an accurate idea of what they sound like.

Each Chinese character is pronounced using only one syllable. However, in addition to the syllable, each character also has a particular *tone*, which refers to how the pitch of the voice is used. In standard Chinese there are four different tones, and in pinyin the tone is marked by placing an accent mark over the vowel as follows:

1<sup>st</sup> tone (high, flat) **mā**

2<sup>nd</sup> tone (rising) **má**

3<sup>rd</sup> tone (down-up) **mǎ**

4<sup>th</sup> tone (falling) **mà**

The pronunciation of each character is therefore a combination of a syllable and a tone. There are only a small number of available syllables in Chinese, and many characters therefore share the same syllable—in fact many characters share the same sound plus tone combination. They are like the English words "here" and "hear"—when they are spoken, you can only tell which is which from the context or by seeing the word in written form.

Apart from **putonghua** (modern standard Chinese), another well-known type of Chinese is Cantonese, which is spoken in southern China and in many Chinese communities around the world. In fact there are several dozen different Chinese languages, and the pronunciations of Chinese characters in these languages are all very different from each other. But the important thing to realize is that the characters themselves do *not* change. So two Chinese people who can't understand each other when they're talking together, can write to one another without any problem at all!

**Simplified and traditional characters**

As more and more characters were introduced over the years by combining existing characters, some of them became quite complicated. Writing them required many strokes which was time-consuming, and it became difficult to distinguish some of them, especially when the writing was small. So when writing the characters quickly in hand-written form, many people developed short-cuts and wrote them in a more simplified form. In the middle of the 20<sup>th</sup> century, the Chinese decided to create a standardised set of simplified characters to be used by everyone in China. This resulted in many of the more complicated characters being given simplified forms, making them much easier to learn and to write. Today in China, and also in Singapore, these simplified characters are used almost exclusively, and many Chinese no longer learn the old traditional forms. However the full traditional forms continue to be used in Taiwan and in overseas Chinese communities around the world.

Here are some examples of how some characters were simplified:

| Traditional | | Simplified |
|:---:|:---:|:---:|
| 見 | → | 见 |
| 飯 | → | 饭 |
| 號 | → | 号 |
| 幾 | → | 几 |

Modern standard Chinese uses only simplified characters. But it is useful to be able to recognize the traditional forms as they are still used in many places outside China, and of course older books and inscriptions were also written using the traditional forms. This workbook teaches the full simplified forms. If there is a traditional form, then it is shown in a separate box on the right-hand side of the page so that you can see what it looks like. Where there is no traditional form, the character was considered simple enough already and was left unchanged.

**How is Chinese written?**

Chinese was traditionally written from top to bottom in columns beginning on the right-hand side of the page and working towards the left, like this:

幸福一点儿也不
难拥有。只要你
常为人着想，带
来欢乐，你会发
觉到那也是一种
幸福呀！

This means that for a book printed in this way, you start by opening it at (what Westerners would think of as) the back cover. While writing in columns is sometimes considered archaic, you will still find many books, especially novels and more serious works of history, printed in this way.

Nowadays, though, most Chinese people write from left to right in horizontal lines working from the top of a page to the bottom, just as we do in English.

**Are Chinese characters the same as English words?**
Although each character has a meaning, it's not really true that an individual character is equivalent to an English "word". Each character is actually only a single *syllable*. In Chinese (like in English) some words are just one syllable, but most words are made up of two or more syllables joined together. The vast majority of words in Chinese actually consist of two separate characters placed together in a pair. These multi-syllable words are often referred to as "compounds", and this workbook provides a list of common compounds for each character.

Some Chinese characters are one-syllable words on their own (like the English words "if" and "you"), while other characters are only ever used as one half of a word (like the English syllables "sen" and "tence"). Some characters do both: they're like the English "light" which is happy as a word on its own, but which also links up to form words like "headlight" or "lighthouse".

The Chinese write sentences by stringing characters together in a long line from left to right (or in a column from top to bottom), with equal-sized spaces between each character. If English were written this way—as individual syllables rather than as words that are joined together—it would mean all the syllables would be written separately with spaces in between them, something like this:

*If you can un der stand this sen tence you can read Chi nese too.*

So in theory, you can't see which characters are paired together to form words, but in practice, once you know a bit of Chinese, you can!

Punctuation was not traditionally used when writing Chinese, but today commas, periods (full stops), quotation marks, and exclamation points are all used along with other types of punctuation which have been borrowed from English.

**Two ways of putting characters together**
We have looked at *combining characters* together to make new *characters*, and *pairing characters* together to make *words*. So what's the difference?

Well, when two *simple characters* are combined to form a new *complex character*, they are squashed or distorted so that the new character fits into the same size square as the original characters. The meaning of the new character *may* be related to the meaning of its components, but it frequently appears to have no connection with them at all! The new complex character also has a new single-syllable pronunciation, which may or may not be related to the pronunciation of one of its parts. For example:

| 女 | + | 也 | = | 她 |
|---|---|---|---|---|
| **nǚ** | | **yě** | | **tā** |
| woman | | also | | she |

| 日 | + | 月 | = | 明 |
|---|---|---|---|---|
| **rì** | | **yuè** | | **míng** |
| sun | | moon/month | | bright |

On the other hand, when characters are *paired together* to create *words*, the characters are simply written one after the other, normal sized, with a normal space in between (and there are no hyphens or anything to show that these characters are working together as a pair). The resulting word has a pronunciation which is *two* syllables—it is simply the pronunciations of the two individual characters one after the other. Also, you're much more likely to be able to guess the meaning of the word from the meanings of the individual characters that make it up. For example:

| 大 | + | 人 | = | 大人 |
|---|---|---|---|---|
| **dà** | | **rén** | | **dà rén** |
| big | | person | | adult |

| 姐 | + | 妹 | = | 姐妹 |
|---|---|---|---|---|
| **jiě** | | **mèi** | | **jiě mèi** |
| older sister | | younger sister | | sisters |

| 四 | + | 月 | = | 四月 |
|---|---|---|---|---|
| **sì** | | **yuè** | | **sì yuè** |
| four | | moon/month | | April |

| 再 | + | 见 | = | 再见 |
|---|---|---|---|---|
| **zài** | | **jiàn** | | **zài jiàn** |
| again | | see; meet | | Goodbye! |

**Is it necessary to learn words as well as characters?**
As we've said, the meaning of a compound word is often related to the meanings of the individual characters. But this is not always the case, and sometimes the word takes on a new and very specific meaning. So to be able to read Chinese sentences and understand what they mean, it isn't enough just to learn individual characters—you'll also need to learn words. (In fact, many individual characters have very little meaning at all by themselves, and only take on meanings when paired with other characters).

Here are some examples of common Chinese words where the meaning of the overall word is not what you might expect from the meanings of the individual characters:

| 明<br>**míng**<br>bright | + | 天<br>**tiān**<br>day/sky | = | 明天<br>**míng tiān**<br>tomorrow |
|---|---|---|---|---|
| 好<br>**hǎo**<br>good | + | 在<br>**zài**<br>be present at/<br>live at | = | 好在<br>**hǎo zài**<br>fortunately |

If you think about it, the same thing happens in English. If you know what "battle" and "ship" mean, you can probably guess what a "battleship" might be. But this wouldn't work with "championship"! Similarly, you'd be unlikely to guess the meaning of "honeymoon" if you only knew the words "honey" and "moon".

The good news is that learning compound words can help you to learn the characters. For example, you may know (from your Chinese lessons) that **xīng qī** means "week". So when you see that this word is written 星期, you will know that 星 is pronounced **xīng**, and 期 is pronounced **qī**—even when these characters are forming part of *other* words. In fact, you will find that you remember many characters as half of some familiar word.

When you see a word written in characters, you can also often see how the word came to mean what it does. For example, **xīng qī** is 星期 which literally means "star period". This will help you to remember both the word *and* the two individual characters.

**What is a stroke count?**
Each Chinese character is made up of a number of pen or brush strokes. Each individual stroke is the mark made by a pen or brush before lifting it off the paper to write the next stroke. Strokes come in various shapes and sizes—a stroke can be a straight line, a curve, a bent line, a line with

a hook, or a dot. There is a traditional and very specific way that every character should be written. The order and direction of the strokes are both important if the character is to have the correct appearance.

What counts as a stroke is determined by tradition and is not always obvious. For example, the small box that often appears as part of a character (like the one on page 32, in the character 名) counts as three strokes, not four! (This is because a single stroke is traditionally used to write the top and right-hand sides of the box).

All this may sound rather pedantic but it is well worth learning how to write the characters correctly and with the correct number of strokes. One reason is that knowing how to count the strokes correctly is useful for looking up characters in dictionaries, as you'll see later.

This book shows you how to write characters stroke by stroke, and once you get the feel of it you'll very quickly learn how to work out the stroke count of a character you haven't met before, and get it right!

**What are radicals?**
Although the earliest characters were simple drawings, most characters are complex with two or more parts. And you'll find that some simple characters appear over and over again as parts of many complex characters. Have a look at these five characters:

> 她  she
> 妈  mother
> 姐  older sister
> 好  good
> 姓  surname

All five of these characters have the same component on the left-hand side: 女, which means "woman". This component gives a clue to the meaning of the character, and is called the "radical". As you can see, most of these five characters have something to do with the idea of "woman", but as you can also see, it's not a totally reliable way of guessing the meaning of a character. (Meanings of characters are something you just have to learn, without much help from their component parts).

Unfortunately the radical isn't always on the left-hand side of a character. Sometimes it's on the right, or on the top, or on the bottom. Here are some examples:

| Character | Radical | Position of radical |
|---|---|---|
| 都 | 阝 | right |
| 星 | 日 | top |
| 您 | 心 | bottom |
| 这 | 辶 | left and bottom |

Because it's not always easy to tell what the radical is for a particular character, it's given explicitly in a separate box for each of the characters in this book. However, as you learn more and more characters, you'll find that you can often guess the radical just by looking at a character.

Why bother with radicals? Well, for hundreds of years Chinese dictionaries have used the radical component of each character as a way of indexing them. All characters, even the really simple ones, are assigned to one radical or another so that they can be placed within the index of a Chinese dictionary (see the next section).

Incidentally, when you take away the radical, what's left is often a clue to the *pronunciation* of the character (this remainder is called the "phonetic component"). For example, 吗 and 妈 are formed by adding different radicals to the character 马 "horse" which is pronounced **mǎ**. Now 吗 is pronounced **ma** and 妈 is pronounced **ma**, so you can see that these two characters have inherited their pronunciations from the phonetic component 马. Unfortunately these "phonetic components" aren't very dependable: for example 也 on its own is pronounced **yě** but 他 and 她 are both pronounced **tā**.

**How do I find a character in an index or a dictionary?**
This is a question lots of people ask, and the answer varies according to the type of dictionary you are using. Many dictionaries today are organized alphabetically by pronunciation. So if you want to look up a character in a dictionary and you know its pronunciation, then it's easy. It's when you don't know the pronunciation of a character that there's a problem, since there is no alphabetical order for characters like there is for English words.

If you don't know the pronunciation of a character, then you will need to use a radical index (which is why radicals are useful). To use this you have to know which part of the character is the radical, and you will also need to be able to count the number of strokes that make up the character. To look up 姓, for example, 女 is the radical (which has 3 strokes) and the remaining part 生 has 5 strokes. So first you find the radical 女 amongst the 3-stroke radicals in the radical index. Then, since there are lots of characters under 女, look for 姓 in the section which lists all the 女 characters which have 5-stroke remainders.

This workbook has both a Hanyu Pinyin index and a radical index. Why not get used to how these indexes work by picking a character in the book and seeing if you can find it in both of the indexes?

Many dictionaries also have a pure stroke count index (i.e. ignoring the radical). This is useful if you cannot figure out what the radical of the character is. To use this you must count up all the strokes in the character as a whole and then look the character up under that number (so you would look up 姓 under 8 strokes). As you can imagine, this type of index can leave you with long columns of characters to scan through before you find the one you're looking for, so it's usually a last resort!

All these methods have their pitfalls and complications, so recently a completely new way of looking up characters has been devised. The *Chinese Character Fast Finder* (also by Tuttle Publishing) organizes characters purely by their shapes so that you can look up any one of 3,000 characters very quickly without knowing its meaning, radical, pronunciation or stroke count!

**How should I use this workbook?**
One good way to learn characters is to practice writing them, especially if you think about what each character means as you write it. This will fix the characters in your memory better than if you just look at them without writing them.

If you're working on your own without a teacher, work on a few characters at a time. Go at a pace that suits you; it's much better to do small but regular amounts of writing than to do large chunks at irregular intervals. You might start with just one or two characters each day and increase this as you get better at it. Frequent repetition is the key! Try to get into a daily routine of learning a few new characters and also reviewing the ones you learned on previous days. It's also a good idea to keep a list of which characters you've learned each day, and then to "test yourself" on the characters you learned the previous day, three days ago, a week ago and a month ago. Each time you test yourself they will stay in your memory for a longer period.

But *don't* worry if you can't remember a character you wrote out ten times only yesterday! This is quite normal to begin with. Just keep going—it will all be sinking in without you realizing it.

Once you've learned a few characters you can use flash cards to test yourself on them in a random order. You can make your own set of cards, or use a ready-made set like *Chinese in a Flash* (see the inside back cover).

**How do I write the characters?**
Finally, let's get down to business and talk about actually writing the characters! Under each character in this book, the first few boxes show how the character is written,

stroke by stroke. There is a correct way to draw each character, and the diagrams in the boxes show you both the order to draw the strokes in, and also the direction for each stroke.

Use the three gray examples to trace over and then carry on by yourself, drawing the characters using the correct stroke order and directions. The varying thicknesses of the lines show you what the characters would look like if they were drawn with a brush, but if you're using a pencil or ball-point pen don't worry about this. Just trace down the middle of the lines and you will produce good hand-written characters.

Pay attention to the length of each of the strokes so that your finished character has the correct proportions. Use the gray dotted lines inside each box as a guide to help you start and end each stroke in the right place.

You may think that it doesn't really matter how the strokes are written as long as the end result looks the same. To some extent this is true, but there are some good reasons for knowing the "proper" way to write the characters. Firstly, it helps you to count strokes, and secondly it will make your finished character "look right", and also help you to read other people's hand-written characters later on. It's better in the long run to learn the correct method of writing the characters from the beginning because, as with so many other things, once you get into "bad" habits it can be very hard to break them!

If you are left-handed, just use your left hand as normal, but still make sure you use the correct stroke order and directions when writing the strokes. For example, draw your horizontal strokes left to right, even if it feels more natural to draw them right to left.

For each Chinese character there is a fixed, correct order in which to write the strokes. But these "stroke orders" do follow some fairly general rules. The main thing to remember is:

- Generally work left to right and top to bottom.

Some other useful guidelines are:
- Horizontal lines are written before vertical ones (see 十, page 19);
- Lines that slope down and to the left are written before those that slope down and to the right (see 文, page 41);
- A central part or vertical line is written before symmetrical or smaller lines at the sides (see 小, page 47);
- The top and sides of an outer box are written first, then whatever is inside the box, then the bottom is written last to "close" it (see 国, page 56).

As you work through the book you'll see these rules in action and get a feel for them, and you'll know how to draw virtually any Chinese character without having to be shown.

### Practice, practice, practice!

Your first attempts at writing will be awkward, but as with most things you'll get better with practice. That's why there are lots of squares for you to use. And don't be too hard on yourself (we all draw clumsy-looking characters when we start); just give yourself plenty of time and practice. After a while, you'll be able to look back at your early attempts and compare them with your most recent ones, and see just how much you've improved.

After writing the same character a number of times (a row or two at most), move on to another one. Don't fill up the whole page at one sitting! Then, after writing several other characters, come back later and do a few more of the first one. Can you remember the stroke order without having to look at the diagram?

Finally, try writing out sentences, or lines of different characters, on ordinary paper. To begin with you can mark out squares to write in if you want to, but after that simply imagine the squares and try to keep your characters all equally sized and equally spaced.

Have fun, and remember—the more you practice writing the characters the easier it gets!

| | | common words | | | | 1 stroke | |
|---|---|---|---|---|---|---|---|

一

**yī** one; single; a(n)

一个 **yí ge**  a(n); one (of something)
一次 **yí cì**  once
一同／一起 **yī tóng/yī qǐ**  together
一月 **yí yuè**  January
十一 **shí yī**  eleven
第一 **dì yī**  first
星期一 **xīng qī yī**  Monday

radical

一

| 一 | 一 | 一 | 一 | | | | |
|---|---|---|---|---|---|---|---|
| | | | | | | | |
| | | | | | | | |
| | | | | | | | |
| | | | | | | | |
| | | | | | | | |
| | | | | | | | |
| | | | | | | | |
| | | | | | | | |

| | common words | | | | | | 2 strokes |
| --- | --- | --- | --- | --- | --- | --- | --- |

二

**èr** two (number)

**common words**

二十　**èr shí** twenty
二妹　**èr mèi** second younger sister
二月　**èr yuè** February
二手　**èr shǒu** secondhand (adj.)
十二　**shí èr** twelve
第二　**dì èr** second
星期二　**xīng qī èr** Tuesday

**2 strokes**

radical

一

三

**sān** three

**common words**

三十　**sān shí**　thirty
三月　**sān yuè**　March
三个月　**sān ge yuè**　three months
三明治　**sān míng zhì**　sandwich
十三　**shí sān**　thirteen
第三　**dì sān**　third
星期三　**xīng qī sān**　Wednesday

| | | | | | | | |
|---|---|---|---|---|---|---|---|
| 一 | 二 | 三 | 三 | 三 | 三 | | |
| | | | | | | | |
| | | | | | | | |
| | | | | | | | |
| | | | | | | | |
| | | | | | | | |
| | | | | | | | |
| | | | | | | | |

四

**sì** four

common words

四十 **sì shí** forty
四百 **sì bǎi** four hundred
四月 **sì yuè** April
四处 **sì chù** everywhere
十四 **shí sì** fourteen
第四 **dì sì** fourth
星期四 **xīng qī sì** Thursday

| | | |
|---|---|---|
| 五 <br> **wǔ** five | **common words** <br> 五十 **wǔ shí** fifty <br> 五月 **wǔ yuè** May <br> 五年 **wǔ nián** five years <br> 五本 **wǔ běn** five (books) <br> 十五 **shí wǔ** fifteen <br> 第五 **dì wǔ** fifth <br> 星期五 **xīng qī wǔ** Friday | **4 strokes** <br><br> radical <br> 一 |

| 一 | 丆 | 五 | 五 | 五 | 五 | 五 | |
|---|---|---|---|---|---|---|---|
| | | | | | | | |
| | | | | | | | |
| | | | | | | | |
| | | | | | | | |
| | | | | | | | |
| | | | | | | | |
| | | | | | | | |

六

**liù** six

**common words**

六十三 **liù shí sān** sixty-three
六月 **liù yuè** June
六个月 **liù ge yuè** six months
六天 **liù tiān** six days
十六 **shí liù** sixteen
第六 **dì liù** sixth
星期六 **xīng qī liù** Saturday

七

**qī** seven

**common words**

七十七　**qī shí qī** seventy-seven
七百　**qī bǎi** seven hundred
七月　**qī yuè** July
十七　**shí qī** seventeen
七七八八　**qī qī bā bā** almost complete
七上八下　**qī shàng bā xià** worry; anxious
第七　**dì qī** seventh

**2 strokes**

radical

一

一 七 七 七 七

八

**bā** eight

八十二 **bā shí èr** eighty-two
八百零五 **bā bǎi líng wǔ** eight-hundred and five
八月 **bā yuè** August
八成 **bā chéng** 80 per cent
八折 **bā zhé** 20 per cent discount
十八 **shí bā** eighteen
第八 **dì bā** eighth

# 九

**jiǔ** nine

**common words**

九十八　**jiǔ shí bā**　ninety-eight
九百一十　**jiǔ bǎi yí shí**　nine-hundred and ten
九月　**jiǔ yuè**　September
九号　**jiǔ hào**　number/size nine; ninth (of a month)
九分　**jiǔ fēn**　nine points
十九　**shí jiǔ**　nineteen
第九　**dì jiǔ**　ninth

**2 strokes**

radical
丿

丿¹　九²　九　九　九

18

十

**shí** ten

2 strokes

radical

十

common words

十月　**shí yuè** October
十一月　**shí yī yuè** November
十二月　**shí èr yuè** December
十分　**shí fēn** 1. ten points 2. very
十全十美　**shí quán shí měi** perfect; ideal
第十　**dì shí** tenth

你

**nǐ** you

common words

你好　**nǐ hǎo**　How do you do?

你的　**nǐ de**　your; yours

你们　**nǐ men**　you (plural)

你们的　**nǐ men de**　your; yours (plural)

亻 ¹　亻 ²　亻 ³　你 ⁴　你 ⁵　你 ⁶　你 ⁷　你

你　你

您

**nín** you (polite)

**common words**

您好 **nín hǎo** How do you do? (polite)
您早 **nín zǎo** Good morning!
您贵姓? **nín guì xìng** your family name?

**11 strokes**

radical

心

ノ1　イ2　イ′3　你4　你5　你6　你7　你8

您9　您10　您11　您　您　您

21

好

**hǎo/hào** 1. good
2. alright 3. like

**common words**

好啊! **hǎo a** Good!; OK!
好看 **hǎo kàn** 1. good show 2. good looking
好久 **hǎo jiǔ** a long time
很好 **hěn hǎo** very good
还好 **hái hǎo** still alright
那好 **nà hǎo** alright then ... (agreeing to a suggestion)
爱好 **ài hào** hobby, interest in something

# 请

**qǐng** 1. please
2. to invite

请问 **qǐng wèn** May I ask ...?
请坐 **qǐng zuò** Please sit down.
请进 **qǐng jìn** Please come in.
请客 **qǐng kè** play host; treat
请教 **qǐng jiào** seek advice
请假 **qǐng jià** take leave

**10 strokes**

radical

讠

traditional form

請

| | | | | | | | |
|---|---|---|---|---|---|---|---|
| 丶 | 讠 | 讠 | 讠 | 讠 | 请 | 请 | 请 |
| 请 | 请 | 请 | 请 | 请 | | | |
| | | | | | | | |
| | | | | | | | |
| | | | | | | | |
| | | | | | | | |
| | | | | | | | |
| | | | | | | | |

问

**wèn** ask

问好 **wèn hǎo** say hello to...
问题 **wèn tí** question; problem
问答 **wèn dá** question and answer
学问 **xué wèn** knowledge
访问 **fǎng wèn** 1. visit 2. interview

**6 strokes**

radical

门

traditional form

問

贵

**guì** 1. honorable
2. expensive; valuable

**common words**

贵姓 **guì xìng** your honorable surname?
贵人 **guì rén** respected person
贵客/贵宾 **guì kè/guì bīn** distinguished guest; VIP
太贵了 **tài guì le** too expensive
名贵 **míng guì** valuable

**9 strokes**

**radical**
贝

**traditional form**
貴

| | | | | | | | |
|---|---|---|---|---|---|---|---|
| 丶 | 冖 | 口 | 中 | 虫 | 丰 | 贵 | 贵 |
| 贵 | 贵 | 贵 | 贵 | | | | |
| | | | | | | | |
| | | | | | | | |
| | | | | | | | |
| | | | | | | | |
| | | | | | | | |
| | | | | | | | |

姓

**xìng** surname

姓名　**xìng míng**　full name
同姓　**tóng xìng**　having the same surname
老百姓　**lǎo bǎi xìng**　common people

**8 strokes**

radical

女

| | | | | | | | |
|---|---|---|---|---|---|---|---|
| 丨 | 𡿨 | 女 | 女 | 女 | 姓 | 姓 | 姓 |

| 姓 | 姓 | 姓 | | | | | |
|---|---|---|---|---|---|---|---|
| | | | | | | | |
| | | | | | | | |
| | | | | | | | |
| | | | | | | | |
| | | | | | | | |
| | | | | | | | |
| | | | | | | | |

他

**tā** he

**common words**

他的　**tā de**　his
他们　**tā men**　they; them (male)
他们的　**tā men de**　their; theirs (male)
他人／其他人　**tā rén/qí tā rén**　other people
其他　**qí tā**　other

5 strokes

radical

人（亻）

| 亻 | 亻 | 仴 | 仴 | 他 | 他 | 他 | 他 |
|---|---|---|---|---|---|---|---|

# 她

**tā** she

**common words**

她的　**tā de**　hers
她们　**tā men**　they; them (female)
她们的　**tā men de**　their; theirs (female)

**6 strokes**

radical

女

叫

**jiào**　1. call; be called
　　2. shout　3. order

**common words**

叫门　**jiào mén**　call at the door
叫好　**jiào hǎo**　cheer
叫喊　**jiào hǎn**　shout; yell
叫做　**jiào zuò**　be called
叫车　**jiào chē**　order a cab
大叫　**dà jiào**　call out loudly

**5 strokes**

**radical**

口

| | | | | | | | |
|---|---|---|---|---|---|---|---|
| 丨 | 口 | 口 | 叫 | 叫 | 叫 | 叫 | 叫 |
| | | | | | | | |
| | | | | | | | |
| | | | | | | | |
| | | | | | | | |
| | | | | | | | |
| | | | | | | | |
| | | | | | | | |
| | | | | | | | |

# 什

**shén/shí** 1. mixed
2. tenth (mathematics)

**common words**

什么  **shén me**  what
什么的  **shén me de**  etc; so on...
什么时候?  **shén me shí hòu**  when?; at what time?

**4 strokes**

**radical**

人（亻）

| ノ¹ | 亻² | 仁³ | 什⁴ | 什 | 什 | 什 | |
|---|---|---|---|---|---|---|---|
| | | | | | | | |
| | | | | | | | |
| | | | | | | | |
| | | | | | | | |
| | | | | | | | |
| | | | | | | | |
| | | | | | | | |

么

**me** interrogative particle

什么 **shén me** what
怎么 **zěn me** how
那么 **nà me** in that way; so...
多么 **duō me** no matter how
为什么？ **wèi shén me** why?

3 strokes

radical
厶

traditional form
麼

丿 么 么 么 么 么

31

名

**míng** 1. name
2. fame

radical

夕

common words

名字　**míng zi**　name
名叫　**míng jiào**　named
名人　**míng rén**　celebrity; famous person
同名　**tóng míng**　having the same name
出名　**chū míng**　become famous; well-known
第一名　**dì yī míng**　first in position

| | | | | | | | |
|---|---|---|---|---|---|---|---|
| ⼃ | 夕 | 夕 | 夕 | 名 | 名 | 名 | 名 |
| 名 | | | | | | | |

字

**zì** written character

| common words | 6 strokes |
| --- | --- |
| 字母 **zì mǔ** letter (alphabet) | radical |
| 字典 **zì diǎn** dictionary | 宀 |
| 十字 **shí zì** cross | |
| 汉字 **hàn zì** Chinese (Han) character | |
| 写字 **xiě zì** write word | |
| 生字 **shēng zì** new word | |

# 我

**wǒ** I; me

| | |
|---|---|
| **common words** | **7 strokes** |
| 我的 **wǒ de** my; mine | |
| 我们 **wǒ men** we; us | **radical** |
| 我国 **wǒ guó** our country | 戈 |
| 我家 **wǒ jiā** my family; my home | |
| 自我 **zì wǒ** self | |

是

**shì** to be; yes

common words

是的 **shì de** yes
是啊 **shì a** yes; yeah
是不是 **shì bu shì** to be or not to be
不是 **bú shi** 1. not to be; no 2. fault
还是 **hái shì** or
老是 **lǎo shì** always

9 strokes

radical

日

| | | | | | | | |
|---|---|---|---|---|---|---|---|
| 丨 | 冂 | 日 | 日 | 旦 | 早 | 早 | 是 |
| 是 | 是 | 是 | 是 | | | | |

大

**dà** big; great

大声点 **dà shēng diǎn** louder
大家 **dà jiā** everybody
大不了 **dà bu liǎo** at the worst
大多／大都／大半 **dà duō/dà dū/dà bàn** mostly
大小 **dà xiǎo** size
大概 **dà gài** probably
自大 **zì dà** proud; arrogant

一 丆 大 大 大 大

学

**xué** learn

common words

学会　**xué huì**　learned; mastered
学习　**xué xí**　study
上学　**shàng xué**　go to school
放学　**fàng xué**　finish school for the day
开学　**kāi xué**　school reopens
小学　**xiǎo xué**　primary school
中学　**zhōng xué**　middle/secondary school

**8 strokes**

radical

子

traditional form

學

| | | | | | | | |
|---|---|---|---|---|---|---|---|
| 学 | 学 | 学 | | | | | |
| | | | | | | | |
| | | | | | | | |
| | | | | | | | |
| | | | | | | | |
| | | | | | | | |
| | | | | | | | |

# 生

**shēng** 1. give birth; born 2. raw

**common words**

生日　**shēng rì**　birthday
生气　**shēng qì**　angry
生病　**shēng bìng**　fall sick; not well
生吃　**shēng chī**　eat raw food
学生　**xué sheng**　student
先生　**xiān sheng**　1. Mr 2. husband
医生　**yī shēng**　doctor

5 strokes

radical

丿

中

**zhōng/zhòng** 1. among
2. (in the) course 3. hit by

| common words | 4 strokes |
| --- | --- |
| 中国　**zhōng guó**　China | radical |
| 中文　**zhōng wén**　Chinese language (written) | 丨 |
| 中间　**zhōng jiān**　between; in the middle | |
| 中年　**zhōng nián**　middle-aged | |
| 中奖　**zhòng jiǎng**　win a prize | |
| 心中　**xīn zhōng**　in one's heart | |
| 手中　**shǒu zhōng**　on hand | |

# 英

**yīng** 1. related to England 2. hero

**common words**

英国 **yīng guó** England
英文 **yīng wén** English language (written)
英语 **yīng yǔ** English language
英俊 **yīng jùn** handsome
英明 **yīng míng** wise
英雄 **yīng xióng** hero

| 一 | 十 | 艹 | 艹 | 苁 | 苹 | 英 | 英 |
|---|---|---|---|---|---|---|---|
| 英 | 英 | 英 | | | | | |
| | | | | | | | |
| | | | | | | | |
| | | | | | | | |
| | | | | | | | |
| | | | | | | | |
| | | | | | | | |

文

**wén** written language; writing

radical

文

**common words**

文字 **wén zì** script; writing
文具 **wén jù** stationery
文学 **wén xué** literature
语文 **yǔ wén** language (spoken and written)
法文 **fǎ wén** French (written)
日文 **rì wén** Japanese (written)

| | | | | | | |
|---|---|---|---|---|---|---|
| | 二 | 亠 | 文 | 文 | 文 | 文 |
| | | | | | | |
| | | | | | | |
| | | | | | | |
| | | | | | | |
| | | | | | | |
| | | | | | | |
| | | | | | | |
| | | | | | | |

课

**kè** lesson; class

**common words**

课本　**kè běn**　textbook
课题　**kè tí**　topic (of lessons)
课文　**kè wén**　text
上课　**shàng kè**　attend class
下课　**xià kè**　finish class
功课　**gōng kè**　homework
第一课　**dì yī kè**　first lesson; lesson one

**10 strokes**

**radical**

讠

**traditional form**

課

老

**lǎo** old

**common words**

老师 **lǎo shī** teacher
老大 **lǎo dà** 1. eldest sibling 2. gang leader
老婆 **lǎo po** wife (informal)
老公 **lǎo gōng** husband (informal)
老婆婆 **lǎo pó po** old woman
老外 **lǎo wài** foreigner
古老 **gǔ lǎo** ancient

radical

老（耂）

| | | | | | | |
|---|---|---|---|---|---|---|
| 一 | 十 | 土 | 耂 | 考 | 老 | 老 | 老 |
| 老 | | | | | | |

师

**shī** teacher; master

**common words**

师生  **shī shēng**  teacher and student
师父  **shī fu**  master
老师／教师  **lǎo shī/jiào shī**  teacher
律师  **lǜ shī**  lawyer
厨师  **chú shī**  chef

**6 strokes**

**radical**

巾

**traditional form**

師

| 丨 | 丿 | 刂 | 师 | 师 | 师 | 师 | 师 |
|---|---|---|---|---|---|---|---|
| 师 | | | | | | | |
| | | | | | | | |
| | | | | | | | |
| | | | | | | | |
| | | | | | | | |
| | | | | | | | |
| | | | | | | | |

| 同 | **common words** | **6 strokes** |
|---|---|---|
| | 同学 **tóng xué** classmate<br>同班 **tóng bān** same class<br>同时 **tóng shí** at the same time<br>同样 **tóng yàng** the same; alike<br>同事 **tóng shì** colleague<br>一同／一起 **yī tóng/yī qǐ** together | **radical**<br>冂 |
| **tóng** the same;<br>together | | |

# 校

**xiào** school

## common words

校长 **xiào zhǎng** principal
校服 **xiào fú** school uniform
校友 **xiào yǒu** schoolmate; alumni
学校 **xué xiào** school
同校 **tóng xiào** same school
上校 **shàng xiào** colonel

**10 strokes**

radical

木

| | | | | | | | |
|---|---|---|---|---|---|---|---|
| 一 | 十 | 才 | 木 | 术 | 杧 | 杧 | 栌 |
| 杧 | 校 | 校 | 校 | 校 | | | |

小

**xiǎo** small; little

**common words**

小姐 **xiǎo jiě** Miss; lady
小时 **xiǎo shí** hour
小时候 **xiǎo shí hou** in one's childhood
小心 **xiǎo xīn** (be) careful
小看 **xiǎo kàn** belittle; underestimate
小便 **xiǎo biàn** urine; urinate

**3 strokes**

radical

小（⺌）

| | | | | | | |
|---|---|---|---|---|---|---|
| 亅 | 小 | 小 | 小 | 小 | 小 | |
| | | | | | | |
| | | | | | | |
| | | | | | | |
| | | | | | | |
| | | | | | | |
| | | | | | | |
| | | | | | | |
| | | | | | | |

# 朋

**péng** friend

朋友 **péng you** friend
好朋友 **hǎo péng you** good friend
男朋友 **nán péng you** boyfriend
女朋友 **nǔ péng you** girlfriend
老朋友 **lǎo péng you** old friend
小朋友 **xiǎo péng you** kid; child

**8 strokes**

radical

月

| | | | | | | | |
|---|---|---|---|---|---|---|---|
| 丿 | 刀 | 月 | 月 | 刖 | 朋 | 朋 | 朋 |
| 朋 | 朋 | 朋 | | | | | |

友

**yǒu** friend

common words

友人 **yǒu rén** friend
友谊/友情 **yǒu yì/yǒu qíng** friendship
好友 **hǎo yǒu** good friend
男友 **nán yǒu** boyfriend
女友 **nǔ yǒu** girlfriend
工友 **gōng yǒu** fellow worker; caretaker

**4 strokes**

radical

又

| 一 | 广 | 方 | 友 | 友 | 友 | 友 | |

# 们

**men** plural suffix
(for persons)

**common words**

你们 **nǐ men** you (plural)
我们／咱们 **wǒ men/zán men** we; us
女士们 **nǚ shì men** ladies
男士们 **nán shì men** gentlemen
同学们 **tóng xué men** classmates
人们 **rén men** people

**5 strokes**

**radical**
人（亻）

**traditional form**
們

# 呢

**ne** question particle

**common words**

你呢？ **nǐ ne** How about you?

他（她）呢？ **tā ne** How about him (her)?

我们呢？ **wǒ men ne** How about us?

人呢？ **rén ne** Where's the person?

| 谢 | **common words** | | **12 strokes** |
|---|---|---|---|
| | 谢谢 **xiè xie** thank you | | **radical** |
| | 谢词 **xiè cí** thank you speech | | 讠 |
| | 多谢 **duō xiè** many thanks | | **traditional form** |
| | 不谢 **bú xiè** don't mention it | | |
| **xiè** thank | 答谢 **dá xiè** express appreciation | | 謝 |

| | | | | | | |
|---|---|---|---|---|---|---|
| 丶 | 讠 | 讠 | 订 | 讱 | 讱 | 讱 |
| 讱 | 讱 | 谢 | 谢 | 谢 | 谢 | 谢 |

再

**zài** again

**common words**

再见／再会 **zài jiàn/zài huì** Goodbye!

再三 **zài sān** again and again; repeatedly

再次 **zài cì** once more

再不 **zài bu** or; or else

一再 **yí zài** again and again; repeatedly

不再 **bú zài** no longer; never again

见

**jiàn** see; meet

| common words | | 4 strokes |
| --- | --- | --- |
| | | radical<br>见 |
| 见好 **jiàn hǎo** get better (from an illness)<br>见面 **jiàn miàn** meet<br>不见了 **bú jiàn le** missing; can't be found<br>不见得 **bú jiàn de** not necessarily<br>看见 **kàn jiàn** see<br>少见 **shǎo jiàn** rare<br>听见 **tīng jiàn** hear | | traditional form<br>見 |

| | | | | | | | |
| --- | --- | --- | --- | --- | --- | --- | --- |
| 刂¹ | 冂² | 见³ | 见⁴ | 见 | 见 | 见 | |
| | | | | | | | |
| | | | | | | | |
| | | | | | | | |
| | | | | | | | |
| | | | | | | | |
| | | | | | | | |
| | | | | | | | |

美

**měi** beautiful

common words

美丽 **měi lì** beautiful; pretty
美好 **měi hǎo** wonderful
美食 **měi shí** culinary delicacy, gourmet food
美女／美人 **měi nǚ/měi rén** beautiful girl/woman
美国 **měi guó** the Unites States of America
很美／太美了 **hěn měi/tài měi le** very beautiful

9 strokes

radical

羊（⺶）

| ⸯ¹ | ⸯⸯ² | ⸯⸯ³ | ⸯⸯ⁴ | 半⁵ | 羊⁶ | 羊⁷ | 美⁸ |
|---|---|---|---|---|---|---|---|

| 美⁹ | 美 | 美 | 美 | | | | |

国

**guó** country; national

| common words | 8 strokes |
| --- | --- |
| 国家 **guó jiā** country | radical |
| 国民 **guó mín** people of a country | 囗 |
| 国王 **guó wáng** king | traditional form |
| 出国 **chū guó** go abroad | |
| 外国 **wài guó** foreign country | 國 |
| 外国人 **wài guó rén** people from another country, foreigners | |

| | | | | | | | |
| --- | --- | --- | --- | --- | --- | --- | --- |
| 丨 | 冂 | 冂 | 冃 | 冃 | 国 | 国 | 国 |
| 国 | 国 | 国 | | | | | |
| | | | | | | | |
| | | | | | | | |
| | | | | | | | |
| | | | | | | | |
| | | | | | | | |
| | | | | | | | |
| | | | | | | | |

| 人 | common words | 2 strokes |
|---|---|---|

人人/每人 **rén rén/měi rén** everyone
人口 **rén kǒu** population
工人 **gōng rén** worker
大人/成人 **dà rén/chéng rén** adult
本人 **běn rén** oneself
客人 **kè rén** guest

radical
人

**rén** person; people

# 吗

**ma** question particle

**common words**

是吗? **shì ma** Is that so?; Is it?
好吗? **hǎo ma** good?; alright?
忙吗? **máng ma** busy?
行吗? **xíng ma** Is it okay?
可以吗? **kě yǐ ma** May I?
有事吗? **yǒu shì ma** what's up?

**6 strokes**

radical
口

traditional form
嗎

| | | | | | | | |
|---|---|---|---|---|---|---|---|
| 丨 | 口 | 口 | 吗 | 吗 | 吗 | 吗 | 吗 |
| 吗 | | | | | | | |
| | | | | | | | |
| | | | | | | | |
| | | | | | | | |
| | | | | | | | |
| | | | | | | | |
| | | | | | | | |

也

**yě** also; too

**common words**

也是　**yě shì**　is also ...
也好　**yě hǎo**　may as well
也许　**yě xǔ**　perhaps

| | | | | | | |
|---|---|---|---|---|---|---|
| 乛 | 也 | 也 | 也 | 也 | 也 | |

| 不 | **common words** | **4 strokes** |
| :---: | :--- | :---: |
| | 不对 **bú duì** 1. incorrect 2. something is wrong | **radical** |
| | 不要 **bú yào** don't want | 一 |
| | 不会 **bú huì** 1. don't know how 2. unlikely | |

不对 **bú duì** 1. incorrect 2. something is wrong
不要 **bú yào** don't want
不会 **bú huì** 1. don't know how 2. unlikely
不同/不一样 **bù tóng/bù yí yàng** it's different
不客气 **bú kè qi** not at all; don't mention it
不好意思 **bù hǎo yì si** 1. embarrassed 2. excuse me
对不起 **duì bu qǐ** sorry

**bù** not; no

| 一 | 丁 | 不 | 不 | 不 | 不 | 不 | |
|---|---|---|---|---|---|---|---|
| | | | | | | | |
| | | | | | | | |
| | | | | | | | |
| | | | | | | | |
| | | | | | | | |
| | | | | | | | |
| | | | | | | | |
| | | | | | | | |

| 谁 | **common words** | | **10 strokes** |
|---|---|---|---|
| | 谁的 **shéi de/shuí de** whose<br>谁知道 **shéi zhī dào/shuí zhī dào** no one knows | | **radical**<br>讠 |
| **shéi/shuí** who | | | **traditional form**<br>誰 |

| | | | | | | | |
|---|---|---|---|---|---|---|---|
| 丶 | 讠 | 订 | 订 | 计 | 计 | 许 | 诈 |
| 诈 | 谁 | 谁 | 谁 | 谁 | | | |
| | | | | | | | |
| | | | | | | | |
| | | | | | | | |
| | | | | | | | |
| | | | | | | | |
| | | | | | | | |
| | | | | | | | |

的

**de** particle

我的 **wǒ de** my; mine
你的 **nǐ de** your; yours
他的／她的 **tā de** his/hers
谁的 **shéi de/shuí de** whose
有的 **yǒu de** some
挺好的 **tǐng hǎo de** quite good

8 strokes

radical
白

的 的 的 的 的 的 的 的

的 的 的

家

**jiā** family; home

家庭 **jiā tíng** family
家人 **jiā rén** family member
人家 **rén jiā** other people
回家 **huí jiā** return home
每家/家家 **měi jiā/jiā jiā** every family; every household
一家大小 **yī jiā dà xiǎo** everyone in a family

| 爸 | | | | | | | | |
|---|---|---|---|---|---|---|---|---|

**bà** father

| common words | 8 strokes |
|---|---|
| 爸爸 **bà ba** father | |
| 爸爸妈妈 **bà ba mā ma** parents | radical |
| 老爸 **lǎo bà** father (informal) | 父 |

| ⺀¹ | ⺍² | 少³ | 父⁴ | 爷⁵ | 爷⁶ | 爸⁷ | 爸⁸ |
|---|---|---|---|---|---|---|---|
| 爸 | 爸 | 爸 | | | | | |
| | | | | | | | |
| | | | | | | | |
| | | | | | | | |
| | | | | | | | |
| | | | | | | | |
| | | | | | | | |
| | | | | | | | |

# 和

**hé**  1. ...and...
2. harmony

**common words**

和好 **hé hǎo** reconcile
和气 **hé qì** amiable; friendly
和平 **hé píng** peace
和事老 **hé shì lǎo** mediator

**8 strokes**

radical

禾

妈

**mā** mother

妈妈 **mā ma** mother
姨妈 **yí mā** aunt (mother's married sister)
姑妈 **gū mā** aunt (father's married sister)

**6 strokes**

radical
女

traditional form
媽

哥

**gē** older brother

| common words | 10 strokes |
| --- | --- |

哥哥 **gē ge** older brother
大哥 **dà gē** eldest brother
二哥 **èr gē** second elder brother
哥儿们 **gēr men** 1. brothers 2. buddies
帅哥 **shuài gē** handsome man

radical
一

# 姐

**jiě** older sister

radical

女

**common words**

姐姐　**jiě jie**　older sister
姐妹　**jiě mèi**　sisters
大姐　**dà jiě**　1. eldest sister 2. older woman
二姐　**èr jiě**　second elder sister
小姐　**xiǎo jiě**　Miss; lady
空姐　**kōng jiě**　air stewardess

| 1 く | 女 2 | 3 女 | 如 4 | 如 5 | 姐 6 | 姐 7 | 姐 8 |
|---|---|---|---|---|---|---|---|
| 姐 | 姐 | 姐 | | | | | |
| | | | | | | | |
| | | | | | | | |
| | | | | | | | |
| | | | | | | | |
| | | | | | | | |
| | | | | | | | |

弟

**dì** younger brother

**common words**

弟弟　**dì di**　younger brother

弟妹　**dì mèi**　1. younger brother and sister 2. younger brother's wife

兄弟　**xiōng dì**　brothers

姐弟　**jiě dì**　older sister and younger brother

徒弟　**tú dì**　disciple; follower

**7 strokes**

radical

八（丷）

妹

**mèi** younger sister

**common words**

妹妹 **mèi mei** younger sister
大妹 **dà mèi** first younger sister
三妹 **sān mèi** third younger sister
小妹 **xiǎo mèi** youngest sister
姐妹 **jiě mèi** sisters
兄弟姐妹 **xiōng dì jiě mèi** brothers and sisters

住

**zhù** 1. live; stay
    2. stop

common words

住家 **zhù jiā** residence
住址 **zhù zhǐ** address (residence)
住口 **zhù kǒu** shut up
住手 **zhù shǒu** Hands off!
站住 **zhàn zhù** Halt!
记住 **jì zhù** remember

7 strokes

radical

人（亻）

| | | | | | | | |
|---|---|---|---|---|---|---|---|
| 丿 | 亻 | 亻 | 仁 | 仨 | 住 | 住 | 住 |
| 住 | 住 | | | | | | |
| | | | | | | | |
| | | | | | | | |
| | | | | | | | |
| | | | | | | | |
| | | | | | | | |
| | | | | | | | |

71

| 在 | | 6 strokes |
| --- | --- | --- |

**zài** 1. be; at 2. live

**common words**

在吗? **zài ma** in?
在家里 **zài jiā lǐ** at home
不在 **bú zài** not in
现在 **xiàn zài** now; currently
还在 **hái zài** still there
好在 **hǎo zài** fortunately

radical

土

| 一 | ナ | オ | 右 | 在 | 在 | 在 | 在 |
| --- | --- | --- | --- | --- | --- | --- | --- |
| 在 | | | | | | | |
| | | | | | | | |
| | | | | | | | |
| | | | | | | | |
| | | | | | | | |
| | | | | | | | |
| | | | | | | | |
| | | | | | | | |

# 这

**zhè** this

**common words**

这个 **zhè ge** 1. this one 2. in this case; in this matter
这儿/这里/这边 **zhèr/zhè lǐ/zhè biān** here
这些 **zhè xiē** these
这样 **zhè yàng** this way; like this
这么 **zhè me** such, so
这次 **zhè cì** this time
到这儿来 **dào zhèr lái** Come here!

**radical**
辶

**traditional form**
這

女

**nǚ** female

**common words**

女儿 **nǚ ér** daughter
女生 **nǚ shēng** female student; school girl
女性 **nǚ xìng** female gender
女士 **nǚ shì** Madam
女人 **nǚ rén** 1. woman 2. wife 3. mistress
妇女 **fù nǚ** woman

女 女 女 女 女 女

# 儿

**ér/r**  1. child 2. suffix

**common words**

儿子 **ér zi** son
儿童 **ér tóng** child
大儿子 **dà ér zi** eldest son
小儿子 **xiǎo ér zi** youngest son
一会儿 **yí huìr** a moment; a short while
一点儿 **yì diǎnr** a little

**2 strokes**

**radical**

儿

**traditional form**

兒

| 丿 | 儿 | 儿 | 儿 | 儿 | | | |
|---|---|---|---|---|---|---|---|
| | | | | | | | |
| | | | | | | | |
| | | | | | | | |
| | | | | | | | |
| | | | | | | | |
| | | | | | | | |
| | | | | | | | |
| | | | | | | | |

# 那

**nà/nèi** 1. that
2. in that case

6 strokes

radical

阝

**common words**

那个 **nà ge** that (one)
那里／那儿／那边 **nà li/nàr/nà biān** there
那些 **nà xiē** those
那样 **nà yàng** 1. same as 2. that type
那么 **nà me** 1. in that case; then 2. same way
那么点儿 **nà me diǎnr** such a small amount ...

| | | | | | | | |
|---|---|---|---|---|---|---|---|
| 刁 | 刁 | 刁 | 刃 | 那 | 那 | 那 | 那 |
| 那 | | | | | | | |
| | | | | | | | |
| | | | | | | | |
| | | | | | | | |
| | | | | | | | |
| | | | | | | | |
| | | | | | | | |

# 男

**nán** male

男孩／男孩子 **nán hái/nán hái zi** boy
男生 **nán shēng** male student; school boy
男人 **nán rén** man
男性 **nán xìng** male gender
男男女女 **nán nán nǔ nǔ** boys and girls
男厕／男厕所 **nán cè/nán cè suǒ** man's toilet

**7 strokes**

**radical**

田

孩

**hái** child

**common words**

孩子／小孩 **hái zi/xiǎo hái** child
孩子气 **hái zi qì** childish
孩子话 **hái zi huà** childish words
男孩／男孩子 **nán hái/nán hái zi** boy
女孩／女孩子 **nǚ hái/nǚ hái zi** girl

**9 strokes**

radical

子

了　了　子　子　孜　孩　孩　孩

孩　孩　孩　孩

子

**zi/zǐ** 1. son 2. seed
3. suffix (noun)

radical

子

**common words**

子女／儿女　**zǐ nǚ/ér nǚ**　son and daughter; children
儿子　**ér zi**　son
妻子　**qī zi**　wife
桌子　**zhuō zi**　table; desk
车子　**chē zi**　1. vehicle (small scale) 2. bicycle
一下子　**yí xià zi**　1. all of a sudden 2. all at once

了　了　子　子　子　子

| 都 | | common words | | | 10 strokes | |
|---|---|---|---|---|---|---|

都有 **dōu yǒu** all have
都是 **dōu shì** all are
都会 **dōu huì** all know how to do
都市/都会 **dū shì/dū huì** big city
首都 **shǒu dū** capital city

radical

阝

**dōu/dū** 1. all; even
2. big city

| 一 | 十 | 土 | 少 | 者 | 者 | 者 | 者 |
|---|---|---|---|---|---|---|---|
| 都 | 都 | 都 | 都 | 都 | | | |
| | | | | | | | |
| | | | | | | | |
| | | | | | | | |
| | | | | | | | |
| | | | | | | | |
| | | | | | | | |

没

**méi** haven't; without

common words

没有 **méi yǒu** don't have; haven't
没错 **méi cuò** correct
没问题 **méi wèn tí** no question; no problem
没事 **méi shì** 1. free 2. no problem; alright
没关系/没什么 **méi guān xi/méi shén me**
it doesn't matter
还没 **hái méi** not yet

radical
氵

traditional form

没

| | | | | | | |
|---|---|---|---|---|---|---|
| 丶 | 氵 | 氵 | 氵 | 氵 | 没 | 没 | 没 |
| 没 | 没 | | | | | | |
| | | | | | | | |
| | | | | | | | |
| | | | | | | | |
| | | | | | | | |
| | | | | | | | |
| | | | | | | | |

有

**yǒu** has; have

| | | |
|---|---|---|
| common words | | 6 strokes |
| | | radical 月 |

有的/有些 **yǒu de/yǒu xiē** some
有学问 **yǒu xué wèn** knowledgeable
有点儿 **yǒu diǎnr** a little; somewhat
有没有(?) **yǒu méi yǒu** 1. did you? 2. whether or not
只有 **zhǐ yǒu** there's only ...
还有 **hái yǒu** moreover; furthermore

一 ナ 右 有 有 有 有 有

有

# 做

**zuò** do; make

**common words**

做好／做完 **zuò hǎo/zuò wán** finish; complete
做错 **zuò cuò** do wrongly
做人 **zuò rén** be an upright person
做饭 **zuò fàn** cook a meal
做作业 **zuò zuò yè** do assignment
做工 **zuò gōng** work

**11 strokes**

radical

人（亻）

| | | | | | | |
|---|---|---|---|---|---|---|
| 丿¹ | 亻² | 仁₃ | 仕⁴ | 估₅ | 估⁶ | 做₇ ⁸ |
| 做₉ | 做¹⁰ | 做¹¹ | 做 | 做 | 做 | |

| 事 | **common words** | **8 strokes** |
| :---: | :--- | :---: |
| | 事事／每事 **shì shì/měi shì** every matter | **radical** |
| | 事前 **shì qián** in advance; beforehand | 一 |
| | 事后 **shì hòu** afterwards; after the event | |
| | 小事 **xiǎo shì** trivial matter | |
| | 故事 **gù shì** story | |
| | 做事 **zuò shì** 1. work 2. deal with matters | |
| **shì** matter | | |

| 一 | 丆 | 丙 | 亘 | 写 | 写 | 事 | 事 |
|:---:|:---:|:---:|:---:|:---:|:---:|:---:|:---:|
| 1 | 2 | 3 | 4 | 5 | 6 | 7 | 8 |

| 事 | 事 | 事 | | | | | |
|:---:|:---:|:---:|:---:|:---:|:---:|:---:|:---:|
| | | | | | | | |

两

**liǎng** two

两个月 **liǎng ge yuè** two months
两百 **liǎng bǎi** two hundred
两次 **liǎng cì** twice
两样 **liǎng yàng** two types; different
两口子 **liǎng kǒu zi** a couple; husband and wife
没两样 **méi liǎng yàng** the same

radical
一

traditional form
兩

个

**gè** most common measure word

个个/每个 **gè gè/měi ge** each one (of something)
个人 **gè rén** individual
个子 **gè zi** body size
两个门 **liǎng ge mén** two doors
那个 **nà ge** that (one)
这个 **zhè ge** 1. this one 2. in this case; in this matter

**3 strokes**

radical

人

traditional form

個

多

**duō** 1. many, much
　　　2. far more

**common words**

多少(?) **duō shǎo** 1. how many/much? 2. tend to
多大(?) **duō dà** 1. how old(?) 2. how big(?)
多半 **duō bàn** more often than not
多么 **duō me** no matter how
差不多 **chà bu duō** about; more or less

**6 strokes**

radical

夕

少

**shǎo/shào** 1. few; little 2. young

**common words**

少女　**shào nǚ**　teenage girl
少不了　**shǎo bu liǎo**　can't do without
青少年　**qīng shào nián**　teenager
很少　**hěn shǎo**　very little; very few
不少　**bù shǎo**　quite a lot
男女老少　**nán nǚ lǎo shào**　men, women, young and old

4 strokes

radical

小

丨　小　小　少　少　少　少

# 时

**shí** time

时间 **shí jiān** time
时期 **shí qī** period of time
时时/不时 **shí shí/bù shí** often
一时 **yī shí** temporarily; momentarily
有时/有时候 **yǒu shí/yǒu shí hou** sometimes
到时 **dào shí** when the time comes

**7 strokes**

radical

日

traditional form

時

# 间

**jiān** 1. between
2. room 3. measure word

**common words**

时间　**shí jiān**　time
中间　**zhōng jiān**　between; in the middle
房间　**fáng jiān**　room
夜间　**yè jiān**　at night; night time
洗手间　**xǐ shǒu jiān**　washroom
一间客房　**yī jiān kè fáng**　a guest room

**7 strokes**

**radical**

门

**traditional form**

間

90

# 今

**jīn** now; at present

**common words**

今天/今日 **jīn tiān/jīn rì** today
今早 **jīn zǎo** this morning
今晚 **jīn wǎn** tonight; this evening
今年 **jīn nián** this year
今后 **jīn hòu** from now on
至今 **zhì jīn** up to now; so far
如今 **rú jīn** now; nowadays

**4 strokes**

radical

人

丿　人　스　今　今　今　今

| 天 | **common words** | **4 strokes** |
| :---: | :--- | :---: |
| | 天天/每天 **tiān tiān/měi tiān** every day <br> 天上/天空中 **tiān shàng/tiān kōng zhōng** <br> in the sky <br> 天气 **tiān qì** weather <br> 明天 **míng tiān** tomorrow <br> 昨天 **zuó tiān** yesterday <br> 白天 **bái tiān** daytime | **radical** <br> 大 |

**tiān** 1. day 2. sky

| 一 | 二 | 于 | 天 | 天 | 天 | 天 | |
|---|---|---|---|---|---|---|---|
| | | | | | | | |
| | | | | | | | |
| | | | | | | | |
| | | | | | | | |
| | | | | | | | |
| | | | | | | | |
| | | | | | | | |
| | | | | | | | |

几

**jǐ/jī** 1. how many
2. several 3. almost

**common words**

几个(?) **jǐ ge** 1. how many? 2. several (of something)

几次(?) **jǐ cì** 1. how many times? 2. several times

几时(?) **jǐ shí** 1. when? 2. anytime

几天(?) **jǐ tiān** 1. how many days? 2. several days

几分(?) **jǐ fēn** 1. how many points? 2. somewhat

几点(?) **jǐ diǎn** 1. what time? 2. several dots

几乎 **jī hū** almost, nearly

**2 strokes**

**radical**

几

**traditional form**

幾

丿　几　几　几　几

号

**hào** 1. date 2. size
3. sequence 4. signal

common words

号码 **hào mǎ** number
几号? **jǐ hào** which number?; what size?; what date?
十号 **shí hào** number ten; size ten; tenth (of a month)
句号 **jù hào** full-stop
逗号 **dòu hào** comma
问号 **wèn hào** question mark

5 strokes

radical
口

traditional form

號

| | | | | | | | |
|---|---|---|---|---|---|---|---|
| 丨 | 口 | 口 | 旦 | 号 | 号 | 号 | 号 |

明

**míng** bright

明明 **míng míng** obviously
明白 **míng bai** understand
明天／明日 **míng tiān/míng rì** tomorrow
明亮 **míng liàng** bright
文明 **wén míng** civilized; civilization
发明 **fā míng** invent

**8 strokes**

radical

日

| | | | | | | | |
|---|---|---|---|---|---|---|---|
| 丨¹ | 冂² | 日₃ | 日₄ | 助⁵ | 明⁶ | 明⁷ | 明⁸ |
| 明 | 明 | 明 | | | | | |

95

**年**

**nián** year

**common words**

年年/每年 **nián nián/měi nián** every year
年纪 **nián ji** age
明年 **míng nián** next year
后年 **hòu nián** year after next year
去年 **qù nián** last year
前年 **qián nián** year before last year

**6 strokes**

radical
丿

# 月

**yuè** 1. month 2. moon

**common words**

月亮／月球 **yuè liang/yuè qiú** moon
月光 **yuè guāng** moonlight
这个月 **zhè ge yuè** this month
上个月 **shàng ge yuè** last month
下个月 **xià ge yuè** next month

日

**rì** day

radical

日

common words

日本 **rì běn** Japan
日期 **rì qī** date
日子 **rì zi** 1. date; day 2. time 3. life
今日 **jīn rì** today
明日 **míng rì** tomorrow
昨日 **zuó rì** yesterday
每日 **měi rì** every day

| | | | | | | |
|---|---|---|---|---|---|---|
| 丨 | 𠃌 | 月 | 日 | 日 | 日 | 日 |

# 星

**xīng** star

radical

日

## common words

星星 **xīng xing** star
星期 **xīng qī** week
星座 **xīng zuó** 1. constellation 2. sign of zodiac
星球 **xīng qiú** heavenly body; planet
歌星 **gē xīng** singer
明星 **míng xīng** star (celebrity)

期

**qī** period

common words

期间／时期 **qī jiān/shí qī** period of time
学期 **xué qī** school term; semester
假期 **jià qī** holiday
到期 **dào qī** expire
早期 **zǎo qī** earlier time; early stage
上星期 **shàng xīng qī** last week
下星期 **xià xīng qī** next week

12 strokes

radical

月

| | | | | | | | |
|---|---|---|---|---|---|---|---|
| 一 | 十 | 卄 | 甘 | 甘 | 其 | 其 | 其 |
| 期 | 期 | 期 | 期 | 期 | 期 | 期 | |

早

**zǎo** early; morning;
Good morning!

common words

早安 **zǎo ān**  Good morning!
早上 **zǎo shang**  morning
早日 **zǎo rì**  (at an) early date; soon
早晚 **zǎo wǎn**  1. day and night 2. sooner or later
早饭/早点/早餐 **zǎo fàn/zǎo diǎn/zǎo cān**  breakfast
一早 **yī zǎo**  early in the morning
明早 **míng zǎo**  tomorrow morning

**6 strokes**

radical

日

| | | | | | | | |
|---|---|---|---|---|---|---|---|
| 丨 | 冂 | 曰 | 日 | 旦 | 早 | 早 | 早 |
| 早 | | | | | | | |

上

**shàng** 1. above; go up
2. attend 3. previous

common words

上面 **shàng mian** above; top
上来 **shàng lái** come up
上去 **shàng qù** go up
上班 **shàng bān** go to work
上厕所 **shàng cè suǒ** go to the toilet
上次 **shàng cì** last time
马上 **mǎ shàng** immediately

3 strokes

radical

卜

| | | | | | | | |
|---|---|---|---|---|---|---|---|
| 丨 | 上 | 上 | 上 | 上 | 上 | | |
| | | | | | | | |
| | | | | | | | |
| | | | | | | | |
| | | | | | | | |
| | | | | | | | |
| | | | | | | | |
| | | | | | | | |

下

**xià** 1. under; go down
2. finish 3. next

**common words**

下面　**xià mian**　underneath; below
下来　**xià lái**　come down
下去　**xià qù**　go down
下班　**xià bān**　finish work
下雨　**xià yǔ**　rain
下次　**xià cì**　next time
一下　**yí xià**　1. one time 2. a short while

**3 strokes**

radical

一

午

**wǔ** noon

**common words**

午饭／午餐 **wǔ fàn/wǔ cān** lunch
午觉／午睡 **wǔ jiào/wǔ shuì** afternoon nap
午夜 **wǔ yè** midnight
上午／午前 **shàng wǔ/wǔ qián** morning (a.m.)
中午 **zhōng wǔ** noon
下午／午后 **xià wǔ/wǔ hòu** afternoon (p.m.)

丿  ㇒  ㇒  午  午  午  午

吃

**chī** eat

common words

吃饭 **chī fàn** have a meal

吃饱了 **chī bǎo le** eaten; eaten enough

吃不饱 **chī bu bǎo** not full; not enough to eat

吃不下 **chī bu xià** not able to eat; have no appetite

小吃 **xiǎo chī** snack

好吃 **hǎo chī** tasty; delicious

# 晚

**wǎn** night; late

**common words**

晚上 **wǎn shang** evening; night
晚安 **wǎn ān** Good night!
晚饭/晚餐 **wǎn fàn/wǎn cān** dinner
晚班 **wǎn bān** evening shift; night shift
晚点 **wǎn diǎn** be late
起晚了 **qǐ wǎn le** got up late

**11 strokes**

radical

日

# 饭

**fàn** meal; cooked rice

common words

饭前　**fàn qián**　before a meal
饭后　**fàn hòu**　after a meal
饭菜　**fàn cài**　rice and dishes
饭店　**fàn diàn**　1. restaurant 2. hotel
白饭　**bái fàn**　cooked white rice
开饭　**kāi fàn**　start serving a meal

7 strokes

radical

饣

traditional form

飯

| | | | | | | | |
|---|---|---|---|---|---|---|---|
| 丿 | 𠂊 | 饣 | 饣 | 饭 | 饭 | 饭 | 饭 |
| 饭 | 饭 | | | | | | |
| | | | | | | | |
| | | | | | | | |
| | | | | | | | |
| | | | | | | | |
| | | | | | | | |
| | | | | | | | |
| | | | | | | | |

了

**le/liǎo** particle

了不起 **liǎo bu qǐ** fantastic; amazing
对了 **duì le** That's right!
算了 **suàn le** forget it
都上学了 **dōu shàng xué le** all have gone to school
受不了 **shòu bu liǎo** unbearable
吃了 **chī le** had eaten

**2 strokes**

radical

一

| | | | | | | | |
|---|---|---|---|---|---|---|---|
| 了 | 了 | 了 | 了 | 了 | | | |
| | | | | | | | |
| | | | | | | | |
| | | | | | | | |
| | | | | | | | |
| | | | | | | | |
| | | | | | | | |
| | | | | | | | |

# 哪

**nǎ/něi** which; any

**common words**

哪个(?) **nǎ ge** 1. which? 2. any; anyone
哪里(?) **nǎ li** 1. where? 2. not at all
哪样(?) **nǎ yàng** 1. what kind? 2. whatever
哪天(?) **nǎ tiān** 1. which day? 2. any day; someday
哪些(?) **nǎ xiē** 1. which of those? 2. any of those
哪怕 **nǎ pà** no matter

| | | | | | | | |
|---|---|---|---|---|---|---|---|
| 丨 | 口 | 口 | 叮 | 叧 | 叧 | 哵 | 哪 |
| 哪 | 哪 | 哪 | 哪 | | | | |

# Hanyu Pinyin Index

**A**

| | | |
|---|---|---|
| ài hào | 爱好 | 22 |

**B**

| | | |
|---|---|---|
| bā | 八 | 17 |
| bā bǎi líng wǔ | 八百零五 | 17 |
| bā chéng | 八成 | 17 |
| bā shí èr | 八十二 | 17 |
| bā yuè | 八月 | 17 |
| bā zhé | 八折 | 17 |
| bà | 爸 | 64 |
| bà ba | 爸爸 | 64 |
| bà ba mā ma | 爸爸妈妈 | 64 |
| bái fàn | 白饭 | 107 |
| bái tiān | 白天 | 92 |
| běn rén | 本人 | 57 |
| bù | 不 | 60 |
| bú duì | 不对 | 60 |
| bù hǎo yì si | 不好意思 | 60 |
| bú huì | 不会 | 60 |
| bú jiàn de | 不见得 | 54 |
| bú jiàn le | 不见了 | 54 |
| bú kè qi | 不客气 | 60 |
| bù shǎo | 不少 | 88 |
| bú shi | 不是 | 35 |
| bù shí | 不时 | 89 |
| bù tóng | 不同 | 60 |
| bú xiè | 不谢 | 52 |
| bú yào | 不要 | 60 |
| bù yí yàng | 不一样 | 60 |
| bú zài | 不再 | 53 |
| bú zài | 不在 | 72 |

**C**

| | | |
|---|---|---|
| chà bu duō | 差不多 | 87 |
| chē zi | 车子 | 79 |
| chéng rén | 成人 | 57 |
| chī | 吃 | 105 |
| chī bǎo le | 吃饱了 | 105 |
| chī bu bǎo | 吃不饱 | 105 |
| chī bu xià | 吃不下 | 105 |

| | | |
|---|---|---|
| chī fàn | 吃饭 | 105 |
| chī le | 吃了 | 108 |
| chū guó | 出国 | 56 |
| chū míng | 出名 | 32 |
| chú shī | 厨师 | 44 |

**D**

| | | |
|---|---|---|
| dá xiè | 答谢 | 52 |
| dà | 大 | 36 |
| dà bàn | 大半 | 36 |
| dà bu liǎo | 大不了 | 36 |
| dà dū | 大都 | 36 |
| dà duō | 大多 | 36 |
| dà ér zi | 大儿子 | 75 |
| dà gài | 大概 | 36 |
| dà gē | 大哥 | 67 |
| dà jiā | 大家 | 36 |
| dà jiào | 大叫 | 29 |
| dà jiě | 大姐 | 68 |
| dà mèi | 大妹 | 70 |
| dà rén | 大人 | 57 |
| dà shēng diǎn | 大声点 | 36 |
| dà xiǎo | 大小 | 36 |
| dào qī | 到期 | 100 |
| dào shí | 到时 | 89 |
| dào zhèr lái | 到这儿来 | 73 |
| de | 的 | 62 |
| dì | 弟 | 69 |
| dì di | 弟弟 | 69 |
| dì mèi | 弟妹 | 69 |
| dì bā | 第八 | 17 |
| dì èr | 第二 | 11 |
| dì jiǔ | 第九 | 18 |
| dì liù | 第六 | 15 |
| dì qī | 第七 | 16 |
| dì sān | 第三 | 12 |
| dì shí | 第十 | 19 |
| dì sì | 第四 | 13 |
| dì wǔ | 第五 | 14 |
| dì yī | 第一 | 10 |
| dì yī kè | 第一课 | 42 |

| | | |
|---|---|---|
| dì yī míng | 第一名 | 32 |
| dōu/dū | 都 | 80 |
| dōu huì | 都会 | 80 |
| dōu shàng xué le | 都上学了 | 108 |
| dōu shì | 都是 | 80 |
| dōu yǒu | 都有 | 80 |
| dòu hào | 逗号 | 94 |
| dū huì | 都会 | 80 |
| dū shì | 都市 | 80 |
| duì bu qǐ | 对不起 | 60 |
| duì le | 对了 | 108 |
| duō | 多 | 87 |
| duō bàn | 多半 | 87 |
| duō dà | 多大(?) | 87 |
| duō me | 多么 | 31, 87 |
| duō shǎo | 多少(?) | 87 |
| duō xiè | 多谢 | 52 |

**E**

| | | |
|---|---|---|
| ér/r | 儿 | 75 |
| ér nǚ | 儿女 | 79 |
| ér tóng | 儿童 | 75 |
| ér zi | 儿子 | 75, 79 |
| èr | 二 | 11 |
| èr gē | 二哥 | 67 |
| èr jiě | 二姐 | 68 |
| èr mèi | 二妹 | 11 |
| èr shí | 二十 | 11 |
| èr shǒu | 二手 | 11 |
| èr yuè | 二月 | 11 |

**F**

| | | |
|---|---|---|
| fā míng | 发明 | 95 |
| fǎ wén | 法文 | 41 |
| fàn | 饭 | 107 |
| fàn cài | 饭菜 | 107 |
| fàn diàn | 饭店 | 107 |
| fàn hòu | 饭后 | 107 |
| fàn qián | 饭前 | 107 |
| fáng jiān | 房间 | 90 |

| | | |
|---|---|---|
| fǎng wèn | 访问 | 24 |
| fàng xué | 放学 | 37 |
| fù nǚ | 妇女 | 74 |

**G**

| | | |
|---|---|---|
| gē | 哥 | 67 |
| gē ge | 哥哥 | 67 |
| gēr men | 哥儿们 | 67 |
| gē xīng | 歌星 | 99 |
| gè | 个 | 86 |
| gè gè | 个个 | 86 |
| gè rén | 个人 | 86 |
| gè zi | 个子 | 86 |
| gōng kè | 功课 | 42 |
| gōng rén | 工人 | 57 |
| gōng yǒu | 工友 | 49 |
| gū mā | 姑妈 | 66 |
| gǔ lǎo | 古老 | 43 |
| gù shì | 故事 | 84 |
| guì | 贵 | 25 |
| guì bīn | 贵宾 | 25 |
| guì kè | 贵客 | 25 |
| guì rén | 贵人 | 25 |
| guì xìng | 贵姓 | 25 |
| guó | 国 | 56 |
| guó jiā | 国家 | 56 |
| guó mín | 国民 | 56 |
| guó wáng | 国王 | 56 |

**H**

| | | |
|---|---|---|
| hái hǎo | 还好 | 22 |
| hái méi | 还没 | 81 |
| hái shì | 还是 | 35 |
| hái yǒu | 还有 | 82 |
| hái zài | 还在 | 72 |
| hái | 孩 | 78 |
| hái zi | 孩子 | 78 |
| hái zi huà | 孩子话 | 78 |
| hái zi qì | 孩子气 | 78 |
| hàn zì | 汉字 | 33 |
| hǎo/hào | 好 | 22 |
| hǎo a | 好啊 | 22 |
| hǎo chī | 好吃 | 105 |

| | | |
|---|---|---|
| hǎo jiǔ | 好久 | 22 |
| hǎo kàn | 好看 | 22 |
| hǎo ma | 好吗? | 58 |
| hǎo péng you | 好朋友 | 48 |
| hǎo yǒu | 好友 | 49 |
| hǎo zài | 好在 | 72 |
| hào | 号 | 94 |
| hào mǎ | 号码 | 94 |
| hé | 和 | 65 |
| hé hǎo | 和好 | 65 |
| hé píng | 和平 | 65 |
| hé qì | 和气 | 65 |
| hé shì lǎo | 和事老 | 65 |
| hěn hǎo | 很好 | 22 |
| hěn měi | 很美 | 55 |
| hěn shǎo | 很少 | 88 |
| hòu nián | 后年 | 96 |
| huí jiā | 回家 | 63 |

**J**

| | | |
|---|---|---|
| jǐ/jī | 几 | 93 |
| jī hū | 几乎 | 93 |
| jǐ cì | 几次(?) | 93 |
| jǐ diǎn | 几点(?) | 93 |
| jǐ fēn | 几分(?) | 93 |
| jǐ ge | 几个(?) | 93 |
| jǐ hào | 几号? | 94 |
| jǐ shí | 几时(?) | 93 |
| jǐ tiān | 几天(?) | 93 |
| jì zhù | 记住 | 71 |
| jiā | 家 | 63 |
| jiā jiā | 家家 | 63 |
| jiā rén | 家人 | 63 |
| jiā tíng | 家庭 | 63 |
| jià qī | 假期 | 100 |
| jiān | 间 | 90 |
| jiàn | 见 | 54 |
| jiàn hǎo | 见好 | 54 |
| jiàn miàn | 见面 | 54 |
| jiào | 叫 | 29 |
| jiào chē | 叫车 | 29 |
| jiào hǎn | 叫喊 | 29 |
| jiào hǎo | 叫好 | 29 |

| | | |
|---|---|---|
| jiào mén | 叫门 | 29 |
| jiào zuò | 叫做 | 29 |
| jiào shī | 教师 | 44 |
| jiě | 姐 | 68 |
| jiě dì | 姐弟 | 69 |
| jiě jie | 姐姐 | 68 |
| jiě mèi | 姐妹 | 68, 70 |
| jīn | 今 | 91 |
| jīn hòu | 今后 | 91 |
| jīn nián | 今年 | 91 |
| jīn rì | 今日 | 91, 98 |
| jīn tiān | 今天 | 91 |
| jīn wǎn | 今晚 | 91 |
| jīn zǎo | 今早 | 91 |
| jiǔ | 九 | 18 |
| jiǔ bǎi yī shí | 九百一十 | 18 |
| jiǔ fēn | 九分 | 18 |
| jiǔ hào | 九号 | 18 |
| jiǔ shí bā | 九十八 | 18 |
| jiǔ yuè | 九月 | 18 |
| jù hào | 句号 | 94 |

**K**

| | | |
|---|---|---|
| kāi fàn | 开饭 | 107 |
| kāi xué | 开学 | 37 |
| kàn jiàn | 看见 | 54 |
| kě yǐ ma | 可以吗? | 58 |
| kè | 课 | 42 |
| kè běn | 课本 | 42 |
| kè tí | 课题 | 42 |
| kè wén | 课文 | 42 |
| kè rén | 客人 | 57 |
| kōng jiě | 空姐 | 68 |

**L**

| | | |
|---|---|---|
| lǎo | 老 | 43 |
| lǎo bà | 老爸 | 64 |
| lǎo bǎi xìng | 老百姓 | 26 |
| lǎo dà | 老大 | 43 |
| lǎo gōng | 老公 | 43 |
| lǎo péng you | 老朋友 | 48 |
| lǎo po | 老婆 | 43 |
| lǎo pó po | 老婆婆 | 43 |

# Radical Index

**1 stroke**

[一]

| | | |
|---|---|---|
| 一 | yī | 10 |
| 二 | èr | 11 |
| 七 | qī | 16 |
| 三 | sān | 12 |
| 下 | xià | 103 |
| 五 | wǔ | 14 |
| 不 | bù | 60 |
| 再 | zài | 53 |
| 两 | liǎng | 85 |
| 哥 | gē | 67 |
| 事 | shì | 84 |

[丨]

| | | |
|---|---|---|
| 中 | zhōng/zhòng | 39 |

[丿]

| | | |
|---|---|---|
| 九 | jiǔ | 18 |
| 生 | shēng | 38 |
| 年 | nián | 96 |

[乛]

| | | |
|---|---|---|
| 了 | le/liǎo | 108 |
| 也 | yě | 59 |

**2 strokes**

[卜]

| | | |
|---|---|---|
| 上 | shàng | 102 |

[十]

| | | |
|---|---|---|
| 十 | shí | 19 |
| 午 | wǔ | 104 |

[冂]

| | | |
|---|---|---|
| 同 | tóng | 45 |

八 [丷]

| | | |
|---|---|---|
| 八 | bā | 17 |
| 弟 | dì | 69 |

人 [亻]

| | | |
|---|---|---|
| 人 | rén | 57 |
| 个 | gè | 86 |
| 今 | jīn | 91 |
| 什 | shén/shí | 30 |
| 他 | tā | 27 |
| 们 | men | 50 |
| 你 | nǐ | 20 |
| 住 | zhù | 71 |
| 做 | zuò | 83 |

[儿]

| | | |
|---|---|---|
| 儿 | ér/r | 75 |

[几]

| | | |
|---|---|---|
| 几 | jǐ/jī | 93 |

[亠]

| | | |
|---|---|---|
| 六 | liù | 15 |

[讠]

| | | |
|---|---|---|
| 谁 | shéi/shuí | 61 |
| 请 | qǐng | 23 |
| 课 | kè | 42 |
| 谢 | xiè | 52 |

[阝]

| | | |
|---|---|---|
| 那 | nà/nèi | 76 |
| 都 | dōu/dū | 80 |

[厶]

| | | |
|---|---|---|
| 么 | me | 31 |

[又]

| | | |
|---|---|---|
| 友 | yǒu | 49 |

**3 strokes**

[土]

| | | |
|---|---|---|
| 在 | zài | 72 |

[艹]

| | | |
|---|---|---|
| 英 | yīng | 40 |

[小]

| | | |
|---|---|---|
| 小 | xiǎo | 47 |
| 少 | shǎo/shào | 88 |

[大]

| | | |
|---|---|---|
| 大 | dà | 36 |
| 天 | tiān | 92 |

[口]

| | | |
|---|---|---|
| 叫 | jiào | 29 |
| 号 | hào | 94 |
| 吃 | chī | 105 |
| 吗 | ma | 58 |
| 呢 | ne | 51 |
| 哪 | nǎ/něi | 109 |

[囗]

| | | |
|---|---|---|
| 四 | sì | 13 |
| 国 | guó | 56 |

[巾]

| | | |
|---|---|---|
| 师 | shī | 44 |

[夕]

| | | |
|---|---|---|
| 名 | míng | 32 |
| 多 | duō | 87 |

[饣]

| | | |
|---|---|---|
| 饭 | fàn | 107 |

[门]

| | | |
|---|---|---|
| 问 | wèn | 24 |
| 间 | jiān | 90 |

[氵]

| | | |
|---|---|---|
| 没 | méi | 81 |

| [宀] | | |
|---|---|---|
| 字 | zì | 33 |
| 家 | jiā | 63 |

| [辶] | | |
|---|---|---|
| 这 | zhè | 73 |

| [子] | | |
|---|---|---|
| 子 | zi/zǐ | 79 |
| 学 | xué | 37 |
| 孩 | hái | 78 |

| [女] | | |
|---|---|---|
| 女 | nǚ | 74 |
| 好 | hǎo/háo | 22 |
| 她 | tā | 28 |
| 妈 | mā | 66 |
| 姓 | xìng | 26 |
| 妹 | mèi | 70 |
| 姐 | jiě | 68 |

## 4 strokes

| [木] | | |
|---|---|---|
| 校 | xiào | 46 |

| [戈] | | |
|---|---|---|
| 我 | wǒ | 34 |

| [日] | | |
|---|---|---|
| 日 | rì | 98 |
| 早 | zǎo | 101 |
| 时 | shí | 89 |
| 明 | míng | 95 |
| 是 | shì | 35 |
| 星 | xīng | 99 |
| 晚 | wǎn | 106 |

| [贝] | | |
|---|---|---|
| 贵 | guì | 25 |

| [见] | | |
|---|---|---|
| 见 | jiàn | 54 |

| [父] | | |
|---|---|---|
| 爸 | bà | 64 |

| [月] | | |
|---|---|---|
| 月 | yuè | 97 |
| 有 | yǒu | 82 |
| 朋 | péng | 48 |
| 期 | qī | 100 |

| [文] | | |
|---|---|---|
| 文 | wén | 41 |

| [心] | | |
|---|---|---|
| 您 | nín | 21 |

## 5 strokes

| [田] | | |
|---|---|---|
| 男 | nán | 77 |

| [生] | | |
|---|---|---|
| 生 | shēng | 38 |

| [禾] | | |
|---|---|---|
| 和 | hé | 65 |

| [白] | | |
|---|---|---|
| 的 | de | 62 |

## 6 strokes

老 [耂]

| 老 | lǎo | 43 |
|---|---|---|

羊 [羊]

| 美 | měi | 55 |
|---|---|---|

# English–Chinese Index

## A

a(n) 一 yī *10*

a(n) (of something) 一个 yī ge *10*

a couple 两口子 liǎng kǒu zi *85*

a guest room 一间客房 yī jiān kè fáng *90*

a little 一点儿 yī diǎnr *75*; 有点儿 yǒu diǎnr *82*

a long time 好久 hǎo jiǔ *22*

a moment 一会儿 yí huìr *75*

a short while 一会儿 yí huìr *75*; 一下 yí xià *103*

about 差不多 chà bu duō *87*

above 上/上面 shàng/shàng mian *102*

address (residence) 住址 zhù zhǐ *71*

adult 大人/成人 dà rén/chéng rén *57*

after a meal 饭后 fàn hòu *107*

afternoon (p.m.) 下午/午后 xià wǔ/wǔ hòu *104*

afternoon nap 午觉/午睡 wǔ jiào/wǔ shuì *104*

afterwards/after the event 事后 shì hòu *84*

again 再 zài *53*

again and again 再三/一再 zài sān/yí zài *53*

age 年纪 nián ji *96*

air stewardess 空姐 kōng jiě *68*

alike 同样 tóng yàng *45*

all 都 dōu *80*

all are 都是 dōu shì *80*

all at once 一下子 yí xià zi *79*

all have 都有 dōu yǒu *80*

all have gone to school 都上学了 dōu shàng xué le *108*

all know how to do 都会 dōu huì *80*

all of a sudden 一下子 yí xià zi *79*

almost 几 jī *93*

almost, nearly 几乎 jī hū *93*

almost complete 七七八八 qī qī bā bā *16*

alright 好 hǎo *22*; 没事 méi shì *81*

alright? 好吗? hǎo ma *58*

alright then ... 那好 nà hǎo *22*

also 也 yě *59*

alumni 校友 xiào yǒu *46*

always 老是 lǎo shì *35*

...and... 和 hé *65*

amazing 了不起 liǎo bu qǐ *108*

amiable 和气 hé qì *65*

among 中 zhōng *39*

ancient 古老 gǔ lǎo *43*

angry 生气 shēng qì *38*

anxious 七上八下 qī shàng bā xià *16*

any 哪/哪个 nǎ/nǎ ge *109*

any of those 哪些 nǎ xiē *109*

any day 哪天 nǎ tiān *109*

anyone 哪个 nǎ ge *109*

anytime 几时 jǐ shí *93*

April 四月 sì yuè *13*

arrogant 自大 zì dà *36*

ask 问 wèn *24*

at 在 zài *72*

at home 在家里 zài jiā lǐ *72*

at night 夜间 yè jiān *90*

at present 今 jīn *91*

at the same time 同时 tóng shí *45*

at the worst 大不了 dà bu liǎo *36*

at what time? 什么时候 shén me shí hòu *30*

attend 上 shàng *102*

attend class 上课 shàng kè *42*

August 八月 bā yuè *17*

aunt (father's married sister) 姑妈 gū mā *66*

aunt (mother's married sister) 姨妈 yí mā *66*

## B

be 在 zài *72*

be an upright person 做人 zuò rén *83*

be called 叫/叫做 jiào/jiào zuò *29*

be late 晚点 wǎn diǎn *106*

beautiful 美/美丽 měi/měi lì *55*

beautiful girl 美女 měi nǚ *55*

beautiful woman 美人 měi rén *55*

become famous 出名 chū míng *32*

before a meal 饭前 fàn qián *107*

beforehand 事前 shì qián *84*

belittle 小看 xiǎo kàn *47*

below 下面 xià mian *103*

between 间/中间 jiān/zhōng jiān *39, 90*

**many thanks** 多谢 duō xiè *52*

**March** 三月 sān yuè *12*

**master** 师/师父 shī/shī fu *44*

**mastered** 学会 xué huì *37*

**matter** 事 shì *84*

**May** 五月 wǔ yuè *14*

**may as well** 也好 yě hǎo *59*

**May I?** 可以吗? kě yǐ ma *58*

**May I ask ...?** 请问 qǐng wèn *23*

**me** 我 wǒ *34*

**meal** 饭 fàn *107*

**measure word (most common)** 个 gè *86*

**measure word (for room)** 间 jiān *90*

**mediator** 和事老 hé shì lǎo *65*

**meet** 见/见面 jiàn/jiàn miàn *54*

**men, women, young and old** 男女老少 nán nǚ lǎo shào *88*

**middle** 中 zhōng *39*

**middle school** 中学 zhōng xué *37*

**middle-aged** 中年 zhōng nián *39*

**midnight** 午夜 wǔ yè *104*

**mine** 我的 wǒ de *34, 62*

**Miss** 小姐 xiǎo jiě *47, 68*

**missing** 不见了 bú jiàn le *54*

**mistress** 女人 nǚ rén *74*

**mixed** 什 shí *30*

**momentarily** 一时 yī shí *89*

**Monday** 星期一 xīng qī yī *10*

**month** 月 yuè *97*

**moon** 月/月亮/月球 yuè/yuè liang/yuè qiú *97*

**moonlight** 月光 yuè guāng *97*

**more often than not** 多半 duō bàn *87*

**more or less** 差不多 chà bu duō *87*

**moreover** 还有 hái yǒu *82*

**morning (a.m.)** 早/早上 zǎo/zǎo shang *101*; 上午/午前 shàng wǔ/wǔ qián *104*

**mostly** 大多/大都/大半 dà duō/dà dū/dà bàn *36*

**mother** 妈/妈妈 mā/mā ma *66*

**Mr** 先生 xiān sheng *38*

**my** 我的 wǒ de *34, 62*

**my family** 我家 wǒ jiā *34*

**my home** 我家 wǒ jiā *34*

**N**

**name** 名/名字 míng/míng zi *32*

**named** 名叫 míng jiào *32*

**national** 国 guó *56*

**never again** 不再 bú zài *53*

**new word** 生字 shēng zì *33*

**next** 下 xià *103*

**next month** 下个月 xià ge yuè *97*

**next time** 下次 xià cì *103*

**next week** 下星期 xià xīng qī *100*

**next year** 明年 míng nián *96*

**night shift** 晚班 wǎn bān *106*

**night** 晚/晚上 wǎn/wǎn shang *106*

**night time** 夜间 yè jiān *90*

**nine** 九 jiǔ *18*

**nine points** 九分 jiǔ fēn *18*

**nine-hundred and ten** 九百一十 jiǔ bǎi yī shí *18*

**nineteen** 十九 shí jiǔ *18*

**ninety-eight** 九十八 jiǔ shí bā *18*

**ninth** 第九 dì jiǔ *18*

**ninth (of a month)** 九号 jiǔ hào *18*

**no** 不是 bú shì *35*; 不 bù *60*

**no longer** 不再 bú zài *53*

**no matter** 哪怕 nǎ pà *109*

**no matter how** 多么 duō me *31, 87*

**no one knows** 谁知道 shéi zhī dào *61*

**no problem** 没问题/没事 méi wèn tí/méi shì *81*

**no question** 没问题 méi wèn tí *81*

**noon** 午/中午 wǔ/zhōng wǔ *104*

**not** 不 bù *60*

**not able to eat** 吃不下 chī bu xià *105*

**not at all** 不客气 bú kè qi *60*; 哪里 nǎ li *109*

**not full/not enough to eat** 吃不饱 chī bu bǎo *105*

**not in** 不在 bú zài *72*

**not necessarily** 不见得 bú jiàn de *54*

**not to be** 不是 bú shì *35*

**not well** 生病 shēng bìng *38*

**not yet** 还没 hái méi *81*

**November** 十一月 shí yī yuè *19*

**now** 现在 xiàn zài *72*; 今 jīn *91*

**nowadays** 如今 rú jīn *91*

**number** 号码 hào mǎ *94*
**number nine** 九号 jiǔ hào *18*
**number ten** 十号 shí hào *94*

## O

**obviously** 明明 míng míng *95*
**October** 十月 shí yuè *19*
**often** 时时／不时 shí shí／bù shí *89*
**OK!** 好啊! hǎo a *22*
**old** 老 lǎo *43*
**old friend** 老朋友 lǎo péng you *48*
**old woman** 老婆婆 lǎo pó po *43*
**older brother** 哥／哥哥 gē／gē ge *67*
**older sister** 姐／姐姐 jiě／jiě jie *68*
**older sister and younger brother** 姐弟 jiě dì *69*
**older woman** 大姐 dà jiě *68*
**on hand** 手中 shǒu zhōng *39*
**once** 一次 yí cì *10*
**once more** 再次 zài cì *53*
**one** 一 yī *10*
**one (of something)** 一个 yí ge *10*
**one time** 一下 yí xià *103*
**oneself** 本人 běn rén *57*
**or** 还是 hái shì *35*
**or/or else** 再不 zài bu *53*
**order** 叫 jiào *29*
**order a cab** 叫车 jiào chī *29*
**other** 其他 qí tā *27*
**other people** 他人／其他人 tā rén／qí tā rén *27*
**other people** 人家 rén jiā *63*
**our country** 我国 wǒ guó *34*

## P

**parents** 爸爸妈妈 bà ba mā ma *64*
**particle** 的 de *62*; 了 le/liǎo *108*
**peace** 和平 hé píng *65*
**people** 人们 rén men *50*
**people from another country, foreigners** 外国人 wài guó rén *56*
**people of a country** 国民 guó mín *56*
**perfect** 十全十美 shí quán shí měi *19*

**perhaps** 也许 yě xǔ *59*
**period of time** 时期 shí qī *89, 100*; 期间 qī jiān *100*
**person/people** 人 rén *57*
**planet** 星球 xīng qiú *99*
**play host** 请客 qǐng kè *23*
**please** 请 qǐng *23*
**Please come in.** 请进 qǐng jìn *23*
**Please sit down.** 请坐 qǐng zuò *23*
**plural suffix (for persons)** 们 men *50*
**population** 人口 rén kǒu *57*
**pretty** 美丽 měi lì *55*
**previous** 上 shàng *102*
**primary school** 小学 xiǎo xué *37*
**principal** 校长 xiào zhǎng *46*
**probably** 大概 dà gài *36*
**problem** 问题 wèn tí *24*
**proud** 自大 zì dà *36*

## Q

**question** 问题 wèn tí *24*
**question and answer** 问答 wèn dá *24*
**question mark** 问号 wèn hào *94*
**question particle** 呢 ne *51*; 吗 ma *58*
**quite a lot** 不少 bù shǎo *88*
**quite good** 挺好的 tǐng hǎo de *62*

## R

**rain** 下雨 xià yǔ *103*
**rare** 少见 shǎo jiàn *54*
**raw** 生 shēng *38*
**reconcile** 和好 hé hǎo *65*
**related to England** 英 yīng *40*
**remember** 记住 jì zhù *71*
**repeatedly** 再三／一再 zài sān／yí zài *53*
**residence** 住家 zhù jiā *71*
**respected person** 贵人 guì rén *25*
**restaurant** 饭店 fàn diàn *107*
**return home** 回家 huí jiā *63*
**rice and dishes** 饭菜 fàn cài *107*
**room** 间／房间 jiān／fáng jiān *90*

## S

same as 那样 nà yàng *76*

same class 同班 tóng bān *45*

same school 同校 tóng xiào *46*

same way 那么 nà me *76*

sandwich 三明治 sān míng zhì *12*

Saturday 星期六 xīng qī liù *15*

say hello to... 问好 wèn hǎo *24*

school 学校 xué xiào *46*

school boy 男生 nán shēng *77*

school girl 女生 nǚ shēng *74*

school reopens 开学 kāi xué *37*

school term 学期 xué qī *100*

school uniform 校服 xiào fú *46*

schoolmate 校友 xiào yǒu *46*

script 文字 wén zì *41*

second 第二 dì èr *11*

second elder brother 二哥 èr gē *67*

second elder sister 二姐 èr jiě *68*

secondhand 二手 èr shǒu *11*

second younger sister 二妹 èr mèi *11*

secondary school 中学 zhōng xué *37*

see 见/看见 jiàn/kàn jiàn *54*

seek advice 请教 qǐng jiào *23*

self 自我 zì wǒ *34*

semester 学期 xué qī *100*

September 九月 jiǔ yuè *18*

sequence 号 hào *94*

seven 七 qī *16*

seven hundred 七百 qī bǎi *16*

seventeen 十七 shí qī *16*

seventh 第七 dì qī *16*

seventy-seven 七十七 qī shí qī *16*

several 几 jǐ *93*

several (of something) 几个 jǐ ge *93*

several days 几天 jǐ tiān *93*

several dots 几点 jǐ diǎn *93*

several times 几次 jǐ cì *93*

she 她 tā *28*

shout 叫/叫喊 jiào/jiào hǎn *29*

shut up 住口 zhù kǒu *71*

sign of zodiac 星座 xīng zuò *99*

signal 号 hào *94*

singer 歌星 gē xīng *99*

single 一 yī *10*

sisters 姐妹 jiě mèi *68, 70*

six 六 liù *15*

six days 六天 liù tiān *15*

six months 六个月 liù ge yuè *15*

sixteen 十六 shí liù *15*

sixth 第六 dì liù *15*

sixty-three 六十三 liù shí sān *15*

size 大小 dà xiǎo *36*; 号 hào *94*

size nine 九号 jiǔ hào *18*

size ten 十号 shí hào *94*

sky 天 tiān *92*

small 小 xiǎo *47*

snack 小吃 xiǎo chī *105*

so... 那么 nà me *31*

so far 至今 zhì jīn *91*

so on... 什么的 shén me de *30*

some 有的 yǒu de *62, 82*; 有些 yǒu xiē *82*

someday 哪天 nǎ tiān *109*

something is wrong 不对 bú duì *60*

sometimes 有时/有时候 yǒu shí/yǒu shí hou *89*

somewhat 有点儿 yǒu diǎnr *82*; 几分 jǐ fēn *93*

son 儿子 ér zi *75, 79*; 子 zǐ *79*

son and daughter 子女/儿女 zǐ nǚ/ér nǚ *79*

soon 早日 zǎo rì *101*

sooner or later 早晚 zǎo wǎn *101*

sorry 对不起 duì bu qǐ *60*

star 星/星星 xīng/xīng xing *99*

star (celebrity) 明星 míng xīng *99*

start serving a meal 开饭 kāi fàn *107*

stationery 文具 wén jù *41*

still alright 还好 hái hǎo *22*

still there 还在 hái zài *72*

stop 住 zhù *71*

story 故事 gù shì *84*

student 学生 xué sheng *38*

study 学习 xué xí *37*

such/so 这么 zhè me *73*

such a small amount... 那么点儿 nà me diǎnr *76*

suffix 儿 r *75*; 子 zi *79*

surname 姓 xìng *26*

**T**

table 桌子 zhuō zi *79*

take leave 请假 qǐng jià *23*

tasty 好吃 hǎo chī *105*

teacher 老师 lǎo shī *43, 44*; 教师 jiào shī *44*

teacher and student 师生 shī shēng *44*

teenage girl 少女 shào nǚ *88*

teenager 青少年 qīng shào nián *88*

temporarily 一时 yī shí *89*

ten 十 shí *19*

ten points 十分 shí fēn *19*

tend to 多少 duō shǎo *87*

tenth 第十 dì shí *19*

tenth (mathematics) 什 shí *30*

tenth (of a month) 十号 shí hào *94*

text 课文 kè wén *42*

textbook 课本 kè běn *42*

thank 谢 xiè *52*

thank you 谢谢 xiè xie *52*

thank you speech 谢词 xiè cí *52*

that 那 nà *76*

that (one) 那个 nà ge *76, 86*

that type 那样 nà yàng *76*

That's right! 对了 duì le *108*

the same 同样 tóng yàng *45*; 没两样 méi liǎng yàng *85*

their (female) 她们的 tā men de *28*

their (male) 他们的 tā men de *27*

theirs (female) 她们的 tā men de *28*

theirs (male) 他们的 tā men de *27*

them (female) 她们 tā men *28*

them (male) 他们 tā men *27*

then 那么 nà me *76*

there 那里/那儿/那边 nà li/nàr/nà biān *76*

there's only... 只有 zhǐ yǒu *82*

these 这些 zhè xiē *73*

they (female) 她们 tā men *28*

they (male) 他们 tā men *27*

third 第三 dì sān *12*

third younger sister 三妹 sān mèi *70*

thirteen 十三 shí sān *12*

thirty 三十 sān shí *12*

this 这 zhè *73*

this evening 今晚 jīn wǎn *91*

this month 这个月 zhè ge yuè *97*

this morning 今早 jīn zǎo *91*

this one 这个 zhè ge *73, 86*

this time 这次 zhè cì *73*

this way 这样 zhè yàng *73*

this year 今年 jīn nián *91*

those 那些 nà xiē *76*

three 三 sān *12*

three months 三个月 sān ge yuè *12*

Thursday 星期四 xīng qī sì *13*

time 时/时间 shí/shí jiān *89, 90*; 日子 rì zi *98*

to be 是 shì *35*

to be or not to be 是不是 shì bu shì *35*

to invite 请 qǐng *23*

today 今天 jīn tiān *91*; 今日 jīnrì *91, 98*

together 一同/一起 yī tóng/yī qǐ *10, 45*

tomorrow 明天 míng tiān *92, 95*; 明日 míng rì *95, 98*

tomorrow morning 明早 míng zǎo *101*

tonight 今晚 jīn wǎn *91*

too 也 yě *59*

too expensive 太贵了 tài guì le *25*

top 上面 shàng mian *102*

topic (of lessons) 课题 kè tí *42*

treat 请客 qǐng kè *23*

trivial matter 小事 xiǎo shì *84*

Tuesday 星期二 xīng qī èr *11*

twelve 十二 shí èr *11*

twenty 二十 èr shí *11*

20 per cent discount 八折 bā zhé *17*

twice 两次 liǎng cì *85*

two 两 liǎng *85*

two (number) 二 èr *11*

two doors 两个门 liǎng ge mén *86*

two hundred 两百 liǎng bǎi *85*

two months 两个月 liǎng ge yuè *85*

two types 两样 liǎng yàng *85*

**U**

unbearable 受不了 shòu bu liǎo *108*

under 下 xià *103*

# List of Radicals

## — 1 stroke —

1  丶  dot
2  一  one
3  丨  down
4  丿  left
5  乛  "back-turned stroke"
6  亅  "top of 刁"
7  乙  twist

## — 2 strokes —

8   冫  ice
9   亠  lid
10  讠  (side-) words
11  二  two
12  十  ten
13  厂  slope
14  ナ  "top of 左"
15  匚  basket
16  卜  (上) divine
17  刂  (side) knife
18  冖  crown
19  冂  borders
20  𠂉  "top of 每"
21  亻  (side-)man
22  厂  "top of 后"
23  人  (入) person (enter)
24  八  (丷) eight
25  乂  "bottom of 义"
26  勹  wrap
27  刀  (𠂇) knife
28  力  strength
29  儿  son
30  几  (几) table
31  マ  "top of 予"
32  卩  seal
33  阝  (on the left) mound
34  阝  (on the right) city
35  又  right hand
36  廴  march
37  厶  cocoon
38  凵  bowl
39  匕  ladle

## — 3 strokes —

40  氵  "three-dots water"
41  忄  (side-) heart
42  爿  bed
43  亡  to flee
44  广  lean-to
45  宀  roof
46  门  gate
47  辶  halt
48  工  work
49  土  (士) earth (knight)
50  艹  grass
51  廾  clasp
52  大  big
53  尢  lame
54  寸  thumb
55  扌  (side-) hand
56  弋  dart
57  巾  cloth
58  口  mouth
59  囗  surround
60  山  mountain
61  屮  sprout
62  彳  step
63  彡  streaks
64  夕  dusk
65  夂  follow, slow
66  丸  bullet
67  尸  corpse
68  饣  (side-) food
69  犭  (side-) dog
70  彐  (彑, 彑) pig's head
71  弓  bow
72  己  (巴) self
73  女  woman
74  子  (孑) child
75  马  horse
76  幺  coil
77  纟  (糸) silk
78  巛  river
79  小  (⺌) small

## — 4 strokes —

80   灬  "fire-dots"
81   心  heart
82   斗  peck
83   火  fire
84   文  pattern
85   方  square
86   户  door
87   礻  (side-) sign
88   王  king
89   𦘒  "top of 青"
90   天  (夭) heaven (tender)
91   韦  walk off
92   耂  "top of 老"
93   廿  twenty
94   木  tree
95   不  not
96   犬  dog
97   歹  chip
98   瓦  tile
99   牙  tooth
100  车  car
101  戈  lance
102  止  toe
103  日  sun
104  曰  say
105  中  middle
106  贝  cowrie
107  见  see
108  父  father
109  气  breath
110  牛  cow
111  手  hand
112  毛  fur
113  攵  knock
114  片  slice
115  斤  ax
116  爪  (⺥) claws
117  尺  foot (length)
118  月  moon/meat

## — 5 strokes —

119  殳  club
120  欠  yawn
121  风  wind
122  氏  clan
123  比  compare
124  聿  "top of 書"
125  水  water

126  立  stand
127  疒  sick
128  穴  cave
129  衤  (side-) gown
130  夫  "top of 春"
131  玉  jade
132  示  sign
133  去  go
134  䒑  "top of 劳"
135  甘  sweet
136  石  rock
137  龙  dragon
138  戊  halberd
139  𫩬  "top of 常"
140  业  business
141  目  eye
142  田  field
143  由  from
144  申  stretch
145  罒  net
146  皿  dish
147  钅  (side-) gold
148  矢  arrow
149  禾  grain
150  白  white
151  瓜  melon
152  鸟  bird
153  皮  skin
154  癶  back
155  矛  spear
156  疋  bolt

## — 6 strokes —

157  羊  (⺷, ⺶) sheep
158  关  roll
159  米  rice
160  齐  line-up
161  衣  gown
162  亦  (亦) also
163  耳  ear
164  臣  bureaucrat
165  𢦏  "top of 裁"
166  西  (覀) cover (west)
167  束  thorn
168  亚  inferior
169  而  beard
170  页  head
171  至  reach
172  光  light
173  虍  tiger
174  虫  bug
175  缶  crock
176  耒  plow
177  舌  tongue

## — 7 strokes —

178  竹  (⺮) bamboo
179  臼  mortar
180  自  small nose
181  血  blood
182  舟  boat
183  羽  wings
184  艮  (⻏) stubborn

185  言  words
186  辛  bitter
187  辰  early
188  麦  wheat
189  走  walk
190  赤  red
191  豆  flask
192  束  bundle
193  酉  wine
194  豕  pig
195  里  village
196  足  foot
197  采  cull
198  豸  snake
199  谷  valley
200  身  torso
201  角  horn

## — 8 strokes —

202  青  green
203  卓  "side of 朝"
204  雨  rain
205  非  wrong
206  齿  teeth
207  黾  toad
208  隹  dove
209  金  gold
210  鱼  fish

## — 9 strokes —

211  音  tone
212  革  hide
213  是  be
214  骨  bone
215  香  scent
216  鬼  ghost
217  食  food

## — 10 strokes —

218  高  tall
219  鬲  cauldron
220  髟  hair

## — 11 strokes —

221  麻  hemp
222  鹿  deer

## — 12 strokes —

223  黑  black

## — 13 strokes —

224  鼓  drum
225  鼠  mouse
226  鼻  big nose